# Is My Bible the Inspired Word of God

# Is My Bible the Inspired Word of God

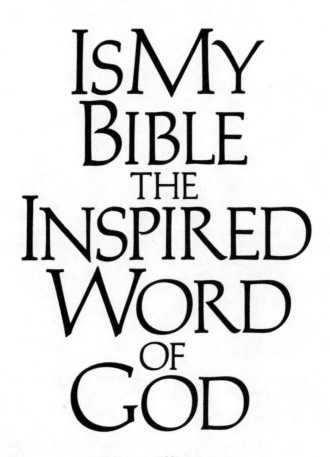

## Edward W. Goodrick

MULTNOMAH
Portland, Oregon 97266

Edited by Rodney L. Morris
Cover design by Paul Clark

IS MY BIBLE THE INSPIRED WORD OF GOD?
© 1988 by Multnomah Press
Portland, Oregon 97266

Multnomah Press is a ministry of Multnomah School of the Bible, 8435 Northeast Glisan Street, Portland, Oregon 97220.

Printed in the United States of America.

**Library of Congress Cataloging-in-Publication Data**

Goodrick, Edward W., 1913-
  Is my Bible the inspired word of God / Edward W. Goodrick.
    p.  cm.
  Includes bibliographies.
  ISBN 0-88070-287-7
  1. Bible—Inspiration.    I. Title.
BS480.G65    1988
220.1'3—dc19                           88-29008
                                                                 CIP

89    90    91    92    –    10    9    8    7    6    5    4    3    2    1

# Contents

# Introduction

"Your Bible is not inspired! In fact, nobody's is, because only the autographs were inspired. That is, inspiration is limited to the words as they were originally written down. Divine inspiration is both inerrant and infallible, and this can be said only of the autographs, the very first copy of Paul's Epistle to the Romans and the very first recording of Isaiah's prophecies. Copies and, much less, translations cannot be inspired, for both contain errors; and translations, being in different languages, contain none of the inspired words.".

The preceding paragraph ought to disturb every pastor, every teacher, every pew-run Christian who loves his Bible, loves to study it, loves to teach it. It disturbs me considerably, especially when it comes from the very champions of orthodox inspiration. Something is very wrong with that paragraph. It leads us to conclude that, inasmuch as it is virtually certain that all of the autographs have perished, we are left with only copies and translations of an extinct inspired Bible. How it must knock the props out from under the simple, believing Christian when he is told that the church has been bereft of an inspired Bible for almost all of its lifetime.

This book is an effort to correct this viewpoint and, by examining the character of the Greek and Hebrew manuscripts that survive and the character of their translation, to restore confidence in the very Bible you and I hold in our hands. It is a corrective that is needed by each one of us. For to the degree that the Bible we hold in our hands is inspired, to that degree is it authoritative. A person who cannot quote Scripture with a confident "Thus saith the Lord" is a shorn Samson.

Most books written to defend the inspiration of the Bible say little or nothing about the inspiration of that particular Bible you and I actually hold in our hands. The authors of these books are called *apologists*, and they often write in response to attacks against the Bible. Since the apologist doesn't defend a segment of the wall not under attack but the segment that is, he can't choose his subject matter. When infidelity attacks the character of what Paul actually wrote or Isaiah actually said, it sets the parameters for the attention of the apologist. This is why most books written today to defend the inspiration of the Bible zero in on the autographs to the neglect of your own Bible, the translation you bought and now read and study.

The inescapable conclusion that follows from some of the statements made in some of these books—namely, that we have only copies and translations of an extinct inspired Bible—is certainly not emphasized when laymen are being taught that the Bible is inspired. In fact, some of our practices are downright dishonest. For it is deceitful to hold the Bible high and proclaim, "I believe God's word is inspired from cover to cover!" while saying under one's breath, "in the autographs." Neither is it a mark of Christian character to lead children in the chorus "The B-I-B-L-E," encouraging them to leap to their feet and thrust the uninspired translation high over their heads while we think of the nonexistent autographs.

These practices occur in churches whose carefully written doctrinal statements assert that the Bible is inspired, inerrant, and infallible *in the autographs*—doctrinal statements written by people trained in Christian colleges, Bible institutes, and seminaries whose own doctrinal statements echo these same beliefs.

The quintessential evangelical statement about the inspiration of Scripture is found in "The Chicago Statement on Biblical Inerrancy." Article 10 begins: "We affirm that inspiration, strictly speaking, applies only to the autographic text of Scripture. . . ."[1]

This seems to me reason enough for a corrective to be placed in the hands of thinking Christians, a corrective that argues, convincingly I hope, that the translation you bought and now use, together with the meaning derived from it, is in truth the inspired word of God and that the children in Sunday school should go right on singing their song.

This book addresses a grave hiatus in our doctrine of the Bible and its inspiration. After an appraisal of the present state of the doctrine (wherein I will suggest a few refinements), I will proceed to pick up where the doctrine has left off and trace inspiration until I have treated not only your own Bible, the one you hold in your hand, but also how you interpret it.

I don't wish to denigrate the work of or appear disrespectful to those who have fought hard and long defending the autographs. I thank God for them. They have done a good job. They are genuine heroes of the faith. So much do I respect their work that, rather than repeat what they have done so well in defending the autographs, I will stand on their shoulders as I develop the concepts in this book. (I do recommend at the end of this Introduction some good books for the reader facing questions about the inspiration of the autographs.) The basic though undefended presupposition of this book is that the language of the autographs, including the meaning derived therefrom, is exactly what God wanted: inspired, inerrant, and infallible.

It will help you get an idea of what this book is all about if you can picture a spring of pure water connected to a faucet by four sections of pipe. The spring represents the mind of God, and the faucet, the mind, heart, and life of the Christian. The four sections of pipe between the spring and the faucet represent in order, starting at the spring, (1) the autographs, (2) transmission (the period when copies and copies of copies of the autographs were handwritten and faulty), (3) translation, and (4) interpretation.

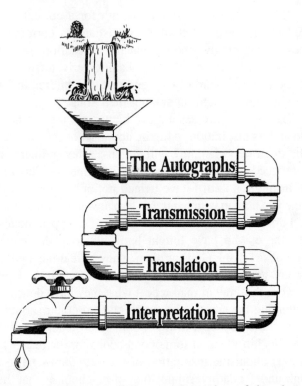

In the chapters that follow, each section of the pipe will be inspected and appraised for intrusions of pollutants. Where pollutants are entering in, I will appraise the efforts to alleviate the contamination; and where this intrusion is alarming or out of control, I will risk a suggestion or two that will help safeguard the water's purity.

My thesis is this: We should all actively labor for the elimination of all pollutants discovered to be in that word of God which we hold in our hands. And inasmuch as inspiration characterizes our Bible both in its wording and in its meaning, and inasmuch as the amount of pollution that has crept into the text is far, far less than the pollution that floods in from our misreading of its thoughts, we must concentrate our efforts to maintain the Bible's purity on how we use it after it reaches our hands.

## RECOMMENDED READING

The following list of books will be helpful for any reader facing doubts about the inspiration of the autographs and for any reader who, though he may have no doubts about the autographs, still is not familiar with its defense. In fact, unless one is somewhat familiar with this, he will have difficulty understanding chapter 1.

### More Elementary Books

Boice, James Montgomery. *Does Inerrancy Matter?* ICBI Foundation Series. Oakland, Calif.: International Council on Biblical Inerrancy, 1979.

*Can I Trust My Bible? Important Questions Often Asked about the Bible . . . with Some Answers by Eight Evangelical Scholars.* Chicago: Moody Press, 1963.

Morris, Leon. *I Believe in Revelation.* Grand Rapids, Mich.: Wm. B. Eerdmans Publishing Co., 1976.

Pache, Rene. *The Inspiration and Authority of Scripture.* Translated by Helen I. Needham. Chicago: Moody Press, 1980.

Packer, J. I. *Fundamentalism and the Word of God: Some Evangelical Principles.* Grand Rapids, Mich.: Wm. B. Eerdmans Publishing Co., 1958.

_____. *God Has Spoken.* Downers Grove, Ill.: Inter-Varsity Press, 1979.

Pinnock, Clark H. *A Defense of Biblical Infallibility.* International Library of Philosophy and Theology, Biblical and Theological Series. Philadelphia: Presbyterian & Reformed Publishing Co., 1967.

Radmacher, Earl D., ed. *Can We Trust the Bible?* Wheaton, Ill.: Tyndale House Publishers, 1979.

Ryrie, Charles C. *What You Should Know about Inerrancy.* Chicago: Moody Press, 1981.

Tenney, Merrill C., ed. *The Bible—The Living Word of Revelation.* Contemporary Evangelical Perspectives. Grand Rapids, Mich.: Zondervan Publishing House, 1968.

Young, Edward J. *Thy Word Is Truth: Some Thoughts on the Biblical Doctrine of Inspiration*. Grand Rapids, Mich.: Wm. B. Eerdmans Publishing Co., 1957.

## Some Grand Oldies

Bennet, Benjamin. *The Truth, Inspiration, and Usefulness of the Scripture Asserted and Proved. In Several Discourses on 2 Tim. III. XVI.* London: L. Latham, 1730.

Gaussen, L. *The Inspiration of the Holy Scriptures*. Translated by David D. Scott. Chicago: Moody Press, 1949.

Gladstone, William Ewart. *The Impregnable Rock of Holy Scripture*. New York: The Columbian Publishing Co., 1891.

Orr, James. *Revelation and Inspiration*. New York: Charles Scribner's Sons, 1910.

Warfield, Benjamin Breckinridge. *The Inspiration and Authority of the Bible*. Edited by Samuel G. Craig. Introduction by Cornelius Van Til. Philadelphia: Presbyterian & Reformed Publishing Co., 1948.

## More Detailed Modern Books

Carson, D. A., and John D. Woodbridge, eds. *Scripture and Truth*. Grand Rapids, Mich.: Zondervan Publishing House, 1983.

Clark, Gordon H. *God's Hammer: The Bible and Its Critics*. Jefferson, Maryland: The Trinity Foundation, 1982.

Geisler, Norman, ed. *Inerrancy*. Grand Rapids, Mich.: Zondervan Publishing House, 1980.

Henry, Carl F. H., ed. *Revelation and the Bible: Contemporary Evangelical Thought*. Grand Rapids, Mich.: Baker Book House, 1958.

Pinnock, Clark H. *Biblical Revelation—The Foundation of Christian Theology*. Chicago: Moody Press, 1971.

_____. *The Scripture Principle*. San Francisco: Harper & Row, Publishers, 1984.

Ramm, Bernard. *Special Revelation and the Word of God.* Grand Rapids, Mich.: Wm. B. Eerdmans Publishing Co., 1961.

Smith, Richard F. "Inspiration and Inerrancy." In *The Jerome Biblical Commentary.* Vol. 2, pp. 499-514. Edited by Raymond E. Brown, Joseph A. Fitzmyer, and Roland E. Murphy. Englewood Cliffs, N. J.: Prentice-Hall, Inc., 1968.

Stonehouse, N. B., and Paul Woolley, eds. *The Infallible Word: A Symposium by the Members of the Faculty of Westminster Theological Seminary.* Grand Rapids, Mich.: Wm. B. Eerdmans Publishing Co., 1946.

Introduction, Notes

1. James I. Packer, *God Has Spoken* (Downers Grove, Ill.: InterVarsity Press, 1979), 143.

# Chapter 1

# *The Autographs— What They Are Like*

*T*he Bible indicates that God has used a variety of modes to reveal himself. And if the Bible cannot be trusted when it tells us what revelations are like and where they came from, then it cannot be trusted at all.

## HOW GOD HAS REVEALED HIMSELF

### Private Revelation

The Bible tells us that God has manipulated dreams (Genesis 20:3-7), has given visions (Acts 16:9), has actually transported spirits to another world to see and hear directly what was happening there (2 Corinthians 12:2-4; Revelation 4-5), has communicated through the Urim and Thummim (Exodus 28:30), and has spoken audibly through angels (Luke 1:26-38) and, once, through a talking donkey (Numbers 22:28-30) and visually, once, by a handwriting on the wall (Daniel 5:5-28). But these revelations are of a private sort and would hardly do for any extensive compendium of what God wanted all to know and heed.

## General Revelation

*Tradition.* God has chosen two means to disperse his revelation generally and for everybody. He talked personally and face to face with our first parents, who related to their children what God had told them. They, in turn, passed on to their children what God had said, and so on. To nonliterary peoples, this art of preserving information has been perfected to an amazing degree. However, sad to say, the Second Law of Thermodynamics works here as it does everywhere else. In layman's language, this law says that things don't fall together, they fall apart. True history slowly develops into myth, something like the parlor game of "Gossip." So tradition is an inadequate vehicle to carry and store God's permanent revelation for any length of time.

*Natural revelation.* Another way God reveals himself to all is through nature.

> The heavens declare the glory of God;
> the skies proclaim the work of his hands.
> (Psalm 19:1)

> —For since the creation of the world God's invisible qualities—his eternal power and divine nature— have been clearly seen, being understood from what has been made, so that men are without excuse.
> (Romans 1:20)

Just as the character and especially the competency of the artist, the inventor, and, most of all, the novelist can be partially perceived through what they create, so we, by studying God's handiwork, can marvel at his wisdom, power, and ingenuity. For the prudent man knows that as water does not rise higher than its source, so a creator, be he an artist, inventor, novelist, or God himself, must be competent to account for all he has created. A novelist cannot create a character and put words in his mouth who is wiser or more intelligent or more learned than himself. In nature there exists thought, imagination, memory, personality. So God must be a being capable of creating thought, imagination, memory, personality.

However, nature, as a source for theology, is limited by the competence of humans to infer from it information about God. Further, inference from nature totally lacks any explicit statements about him. So nature too is an inadequate vehicle to carry and store God's permanent revelation. Something more is needed—a permanent, written record of God's revelation to man in language understandable to man.

## WHAT GOD'S WRITTEN COMMUNICATION IS LIKE

### God Communicates to Us in the Usual Manner

For God, language is an accommodation. Once one feels at home with the fact that the Bible is in the nature of an accommodation, many problems about it disappear. A good communicator—and God is the best—employs the language of the person he is talking to. He uses the words of his listener. And that includes his listener's understanding of the meanings of those words. He accommodates himself to the character of the language his hearer uses and to his hearer's competence in that language. Some four hundred years ago, John Calvin talked about this when commenting on Psalm 136:7 and the creation of the heavenly bodies:

> Moses calls the sun and moon the two great lights, and there is little doubt that the Psalmist here borrows the same phraseology. What is immediately added about the stars, is, as it were, accessory to the others. It is true, that the other planets are larger than the moon, but it is stated as second in order on account of its visible effects. The Holy Spirit had no intention to teach astronomy; and, in proposing instruction meant to be common to the simplest and most uneducated persons, he made use by Moses and the other Prophets of popular language, that none might shelter himself under the pretext of obscurity, as we will see men sometimes very readily pretend an incapacity to understand, when anything

deep or recondite is submitted to their notice. Accordingly, as Saturn though bigger than the moon is not so to the eye owing to his greater distance, the Holy Spirit would rather speak childishly than unintelligibly to the humble and unlearned.[1]

It should not shock us to discover that God accommodates himself to human language, limited and faulty though its wordings and meanings may be. The language people use is as limited and faulty as the people that use it. I can't think of any other way God could have done it, unless he programmed a ROM chip data base in our genes. That, by its nature, would be another way of communicating, but hardly appropriate for rational beings.

As innovative a library as the Bible is, one would predict an abundance of coined words and new definitions to old words to accommodate its new ideas. But such is not the case. The dearth of new words and meanings is nothing less than surprising.

Perhaps the lesson to learn here is that new words and new meanings to old words are not all that necessary in order to share new ideas. Perhaps our propensity to change the meanings of words and make up new ones can be attributed to academic affectation. Or perhaps the New Testament does not deviate from the Old as much as is commonly assumed.

All I mean to say here is that any coinage or meaning change found in the Bible is indigenous to the very nature of any language.

Another area of accommodation is in God's choice of the mode of his communication. When people want to preserve a communication, they write it down. Isn't it quite predictable for a God who has already decided to communicate with man the way mankind communicates to employ man's method of preserving that communication—that is, by putting it in writing?

## What To Anticipate When God
## Is the Communicator

What should a prudent person expect from a document whose writing was strictly overseen by God? I think he would expect it to be true, important, profound, and clear. True because God is true, important because God has said it, profound because God is all wise, and clear because God is the perfect communicator.

*The communication will be true.* What a person says reflects his character accurately. If the Creator of the universe is true, then his word is true and totally reliable. In fact, when you think about it a little, because he is our Lord and we are his slaves, when he tells us something we should believe it even if it weren't true. However, God's word says he doesn't lie, so we will never have to believe such a thing (Numbers 23:19; 1 Samuel 15:29; Titus 1:2; Hebrews 6:18).

As disagreeable as it might be for us to think of God's word in this way, we still ought to. For it teaches us to be submissive to what we discover, regardless of how distasteful that discovery might be.

I admit there is a breaking point to one's credulity—at least there is to mine. For I would find it quite difficult to believe that the moon is made of green cheese even if the Bible right out said that it was. However, I am inclined to back off when I recall that I believe in something even more incredible in the natural world, namely that solid steel is so full of emptiness that it is better to say it is nothing more than electricity. I do not get this from experience. On the contrary, *all* my experience shouts "No" to the idea. Rather, I take it by faith, because nuclear physics says so.

The God who can make the physical universe out of electricity is so utterly beyond my reasoning ability that for me ever to question what he says is nothing but depraved arrogance.

*The communication will be important.* By a quantum leap, what the Creator of the universe says is more important than what the wisest of men have ever said. Therefore the Bible should be studied far more than any other book. The knowledge of a great company of our brightest men has invented the bomb. Only an intense study of the Bible on the part of the world's leaders will convince them that it ought to be uninvented at any cost.

*The communication will be profound.* Because infinite wisdom gave us the Bible, we expect the wisest of us, energetically seeking to sound it, will report "No bottom."

*The communication will be clear.* On the other hand, because God is the perfect communicator, we also expect that "the wayfaring men, though fools, shall not err therein" (Isaiah 35:8, KJV). I also should expect that God will—as all good communicators do—speak in the language of the person listening. So when he speaks to us, he will use our words and wordings and the meanings we attach to those words and wordings. I would not expect him to alter the language any more than people normally do when they must make their language "make do" for new things and ideas.

## God Communicates to Us in the Third Person

The Bible is a library of books, yet contrary to an ordinary library, these books exist in a rough and ready sequence for reading. Everybody agrees that Genesis should come first. And you won't get past the Bible's first sentence without being confronted with a startling revelation about this library's character.

Since it is God's word, I expect him to say, "In the beginning I created the heavens and the earth," a communication in the first person. Instead it says, "In the beginning God created the heavens and the earth." God has given us his revelation in the third person!

The implications of this are remarkable. Someone else or some group of persons was selected to do the writing, not as mere stenographers but, more often than not, as though they themselves were *composing* the documents!

Who were these men? How much did they contribute to the Bible's language and meaning? How did this partnership with God work? And why did God choose to do it this way?

## THE DIVINE-HUMAN PARTNERSHIP IN GOD'S WRITTEN COMMUNICATION

### Who Were These Men?

The Bible calls the people who wrote the Old Testament "prophets." The early church, for good reasons, called those who wrote the New Testament "apostolic men." The prophet was especially endowed with the prophetic gift to mediate God's message to man. The Holy Spirit so operated on the prophet's mind that what the prophet said was exactly the wording God wanted. The Holy Spirit used the prophet's memory or logic or perception or emotions or all of them or none of them (cf. 2 Peter 1:21). The apostles, on the other hand, were given total recall of the message of the New Covenant taught them by Jesus (John 14:26; 15:26; 16:12-15).

The people whom God selected for his partners in this publishing venture were marred descendants of a fallen Adam. They were cursed with his living death and heirs to his degeneration, which pervades one's whole being, mind, and culture, including its language.[2] In spite of this, God chose to speak in the third person.

*There were many of these men.* God also chose to spread the composition of the various books of the Bible over a span of some fifteen hundred years, requiring, therefore, a number of human writers.

Did they all write alike? No, there are noticeable differences in style. We shouldn't be surprised over this, for it goes along with God's choice of the third person mode.

When you think about it, style means quite a lot. It means we must anticipate that the words, their meanings, and the way words are put together will differ somewhat between the human writers of the divine library. We should maintain this attitude even when the present state of the art of literary criticism is, more often than not, unable to articulate these differences.[3] Just as everybody has his own way with words, so the prophets and apostolic men had their own vocabulary and their own definitions for their words. This phenomenon is called *usus loquendi*.

## How Much Did These Men Contribute?

I can't generalize how these men, in contrast to God, contributed to the writing of the Bible. For it varies from one extreme to the other—from the role of stenographer merely recording what God dictates all the way to the human writer doing his own thing and God appearing to contribute nothing except his endorsement that what the prophet/apostle wrote was exactly what he wanted. I say "appearing" because I am not privy to what went on in the mind of either the prophet or God when men spoke, not in the will of man, but "from God as they were carried along by the Holy Spirit" (2 Peter 1:21).

Moses contributed nothing to the first person statement "You shall have no other gods before me" (Exodus 20:3). This is 'dictation inspiration' and is so rare in the Bible that for the moment I can't think of any example other than the Ten Commandments. Perhaps "MENE, MENE, TEKEL, PARSIN" (Daniel 5:25), but that had to be translated. Our Lord, if the account is true, once wrote on the ground (John 8:6). But we don't know what he said.

On the other hand, the statement of 1 Timothy 1:15 is a first person statement different indeed: "Here is a trustworthy saying that deserves full acceptance: Christ Jesus came into the world to save sinners—of whom I am the worst." Here, when the inspired text says "I," the antecedent certainly is not God. It is Paul. I personally don't want God even to have told Paul to say that, for there would be something unwholesome in such a Svengali-like confession. The statement has far greater force when it comes unprompted from Paul's heart and not because God made him say it.

Perhaps the places where God seems remotest are those times when the antecedent to the "I" is not even a prophet but a wicked man, even Satan himself. Whenever the Prince of Liars speaks, we should assume he is lying, even when we read it in the Bible. The only truth to Satan's statements is that those historical events occurred when he actually said those words, nothing more.

Satan lied to Eve when he said to her "You will not surely die" (Genesis 3:4). Even though we may be totally confident that the words were said, the speeches of Acts are not guaranteed to be totally true.[4]

Scripture lies within the range of these two extremes. As the Epistle to the Hebrews puts it: "God spoke . . . in various ways" (1:1). Sometimes the prophet spoke in ecstasy, not understanding what he was saying. Sometimes he consulted documents, sometimes his own memory, sometimes his own wisdom, sometimes his heart, sometimes any combination of any or all of these.

**How Did This Partnership Work?**

After devoting this much time talking about the limitations and imperfections of biblical language, I had better explain how I think God fits in and how what was written down was precisely what he wanted.

*An analogy from Chalcedon.* The hypostatic union of the divine and human natures of the Lord Jesus Christ offers an apt analogy but contributes far more mystery than light on how that partnership worked. However, it does make us more comfortable with that mystery.

*Hypostatic union* is a theological term that identifies how the partnership between the human and divine natures worked in one Person, namely, the Lord Jesus. Using this analogy, we can say, "As a human and divine nature united to form a single person, Jesus, so a human and divine nature joined to produce the Bible."

The Council of Chalcedon (451 A.D.), failing to penetrate the mystery of the divine and human natures of Christ, offered four precautions that would protect the Christian from error when contemplating this mystery.[5] I summarize these as follows:

1. Attribute true and proper divinity to Christ.
2. Attribute true and proper humanity to Christ.
3. Do not so mingle the human and divine that you end up with a being neither human nor divine.
4. Do not dissect Christ so that there are two persons in one being.

Now apply these same precautions to the problem confronting us, namely, how did this divine/human partnership work to produce the Bible:

1. Attribute true and proper divinity to the author of the Bible. It is God who has spoken.
2. Attribute true and proper humanity to the authors of the Bible. They are men who have spoken.
3. Do not so mingle the human and divine that you end up with a different authorship which is neither human nor divine.
4. Do not dissect the Bible so that some parts are of human origin and others of divine.

Except for number three, this analogy is helpful, but it certainly doesn't solve the mystery. And I think we should be warned that trying to probe too deeply would be spiritually hazardous and a presumption so strong as to become arrogant.

*God is sovereign; humans have a will.* Scripture says of itself that "prophecy never had its origin in the will of man, but men spoke from God as they were carried along by the Holy Spirit" (2 Peter 1:21). If this statement means anything, it means that even in those places where human authorship seems to predominate so much that it leaves no place for God—I cited 1 Timothy 1:15 as an example—God is still present. Somehow, without violating Paul as a person, though he thought he was doing his own thing with all the elbow room he needed, Paul was actually being carried along by the Holy Spirit.[6]

It must be true, although I cannot understand how, that the prophet thinks he has willed to say something—and to all appearances he has and we are to take the statement as coming from him—and still, without violating any bit of this, the Holy Spirit manipulates the prophet's thought so that the prophet's will becomes the will of the Holy Spirit.

Great novelists, those who are best at characterization, have sometimes confessed that one of their characters has taken the bit in his teeth and, wreaking havoc with the novelist's plot, has run amuck doing his own thing. I am quite positive that if God would ever write a novel, his characters would never do such a thing, though their behavior would act every bit as though they had.

It comes down to this: If we are ever required to come down hard on one side or the other, then it is the Holy Spirit who wills and the prophet who doesn't.[7]

Call it providence if you like. There exists a divine will that always gets its way. What was written in our limited and faulty language—the angels would say God lisped to us—turns out to be precisely what he wanted written down after all.

I have attempted to address the question "How did this partnership work?" Did I fail? I was afraid I would.

## Why Did God Do It This Way?

God gave us his permanent revelation in a library, the volumes of which he sporadically released through a millennium and a half. Why? I don't know. But I can think of one reason which would be reason enough.

If I were to give the Bible a generic classification, I would call it "The History and Nature of Redemption" and would walk away from my effort dissatisfied because it fails to give the Redeemer preeminence over redemption. I didn't personalize my classification the way the Bible personalizes redemption in the Redeemer.

I have in my library books of theology and its history. They miss the mark by a mile because they depersonalize the subjects. To say that Christianity is more a life is not to denigrate the creed; it is to be faithful to the Bible as it is. Biblical history is primarily biography. And to carry the major burden of New Testament theology, God selected the letter genre, which directly implicates both author and reader in what is being written more than any other literary form.

A God who would do such a strange thing, use such a strange genre to communicate his history of the nature of re- demption, would invite prophets to plagiarize the pronoun *I*. They write about themselves in his name: Isaiah to say, "Woe to me! . . . I am ruined!" and Paul to say, "What a wretched man I am! Who will rescue me from this body of death?" (Isaiah 6:5; Romans 7:24).

In spite of all these efforts to personalize our faith, we still live under pressure to depersonalize it. This might very well be the Christian's chief fault. As long as we are in this condition, we are in no position to question the efforts of God to inextricably meld faith to life by giving us his word as it is, a word that even allows people and their experiences to speak for him.

Chapter 1, Notes

1. John Calvin, *Calvin's Commentaries*, vol. 6: *Commentary on the Book of Psalms* (Edinburgh: Calvin Translation Society, 1849; reprint ed., Grand Rapids, Mich.: Baker Book House, 1979), 184-85.

2. A degenerating race is a concept diametrically opposed to popular evolutionary thinking and certainly contrary to the spirit of our age. It is, nevertheless, consistent with the Bible's view of the effects of sin on the human race. At first glance it may be difficult to believe that modern man, who has learned and produced so much, is less intelligent than his ancestors, especially when one imagines his ancestors to be slouched apelike creatures, lumbering about and grunting. Modern man's achievements have not made him tall. He looks that way because he is standing on the shoulders of his predecessors. Today we no longer produce minds such as Socrates, Plato, Aristotle, Euclid, Moses, or Solomon.

3. Literary critics would hotly dispute my appraisal of the state of their art. But I believe it more seemly that someone other than those who do the work appraise it.

4. However, when the speaker was full of the Holy Spirit, we should be quite confident that he did speak the truth (Acts 4:8; 7:55; 11:28; 13:9). It is strange that we cannot say this of the principal speeches of Acts: Peter's at Pentecost (unless 2:4 can be stretched to reach that far), Stephen's before the Sanhedrin, Paul's on Mars Hill and his defenses in Jerusalem and at Caesarea.

5. Cf. Philip Schaff and Henry Wace, eds., *A Select Library of Nicene and Post-Nicene Fathers of the Christian Church*, Second Series, 14 vols. (New York: The Christian Literature Co., 1890-99; reprint ed., Grand Rapids: Wm. B. Eerdmans Publishing Co., 1952-57), vol. 14: *The Seven Ecumenical Councils of the Undivided Church: Their Canons and Dogmatic Decrees, together with the Canons of All the Local Synods Which Have Received Ecumenical Acceptance*, ed. by Henry R. Percival, 248-65.

6. That is, if you will permit me to stretch the application of 2 Peter 1:21 to both Testaments. If some nit-picker refuses me this liberty, I have only to switch the name "Paul" to "Isaiah" (Isaiah 6:5) and I still have made my point.

7. I am convinced that the church should stop quarreling over God's sovereignty and man's free will. They should brand this as mystery and relegate it to the category which already contains the Trinity and the Hypostatic Union.

This analogy of the novelist's plot versus his characters does not solve the mystery. It does, however, help to pinpoint its location. The plot is predestinated. The characters, although exercising their free will, still fulfill that plot. If 2 Peter 1:21 contributes anything to our understanding of this problem, it is that the downbeat is *not* on the will of man but on the controlling influence of the Holy Spirit.

# Chapter 2

# *The Autographs Are Inspired with No Pollution*

*P*hilosophers have spent a lot of time during the last couple of generations thinking about meaning in language. Hitherto this area of investigation, called *semantics*, had been strangely neglected. My 1948 edition of the *Encyclopedia Britannica* devotes only three lines to the subject, which include an erroneous definition of the term. In the 1977 edition, "Semantics" required eleven columns.

Because God saw fit to communicate with us through human language, traditional statements about the Bible's inspiration must now be refined in the light of our growing knowledge about meaning and words. For now we must make affirmations about the ambiguity of words, about meaning resident in a word's inflection, and about meaning found in the sentence rather than in the word. In short, we need to understand inspiration as an attribute of the Bible's *wording*, not the Bible's words.

## THE NATURE OF LANGUAGE:
## MEANING AND WORDS

### Ambiguity Is a Universal
### Trait of Language

*Grammar is sometimes ambiguous.* Ambiguity is a universal trait of language. Greek and Hebrew are not exceptions. Take an example from the Greek language. Among other functions, its genitive case may be either subjective or objective. That is, the noun in the genitive may be either indicating what is doing the action or what is being acted upon. So when Paul writes to the Corinthians that the love of Christ compels us (*hē agapē tou Christou synechei hēmas*, 2 Corinthians 5:14), there is no grammatical way of finding out whether Paul meant that Christ was doing the loving or was being loved.

There are innumerable examples like this from the Hebrew and Greek Bible. Most of them—the great majority—are not genuine ambiguities but result from our incomplete knowledge of the language and of the culture that used that language.

A remainder of genuine ambiguities in language, I am convinced, are there because language has been corrupted by the Fall. I can't understand how it could be possible for the language of the unfallen to contain ambiguities. C. S. Lewis seems to agree. Ransom, the linguist in Lewis's *Out of the Silent Planet*, found it impossible to translate the ambiguities of his own fallen native tongue into the unfallen tongue of Malacandra.

*Words often have fuzzy edges.* In fact, the more important ones do, such as *happiness*, *feeling*, *meaning*, *ought*, *good*, *beautiful*, *valuable*, *thought*, *idea*, and *imagination*. These words do not lend themselves to the Aristotelian method of description by the use of genus and differentia. Dictionaries must fall back on synonym and analogy.

The person thoroughly infused with the atmosphere of this age is highly resistant to this fact. He, by philosophical fiat, makes the edges sharp or avoids using fuzzy-edged words. It does not follow that because precision is good, one must limit his vocabulary to precise words. The laboratory-trained person finds it hard to think in gray areas. He finds it difficult to appreciate literature and rejects almost all of philosophy and all of theology, denigrating theology's 'godspeak'.

Language is as fuzzy and as precise as the culture it serves. The Bible uses words that are as fuzzy-edged and as precise as the culture its languages served.

Contrary to the philosophical atmosphere we now breathe, what is most important is at the opposite end from the hard sciences on the spectrum of disciplines. These fuzzy-edged, important words reside in history, aesthetics, literature, philosophy, and theology. The better-educated person is at home in these disciplines and is skilled in the use of these words with fuzzy edges. The Bible is rich with them.

*Words often have more than one meaning.* A universal trait of languages is that people often must make do by attaching more than one meaning to a word. The Bible is no exception. Though we are quite happy to translate the Greek *ekklēsia* with the English *church*, it would be misleading to do so where this word appears in Acts 7:38, and it wouldn't fit at all in Acts 19:32, 39, and 41.

A fair sampling of ten pages of the best New Testament Greek dictionary lists eighty-four words. Sixty-one of these have but one definition; twenty-three have more than one meaning (six of which have three meanings, two have four, three have seven, and one has nine meanings). According to Jan de Waard and Eugene A. Nida, "in a dictionary of the Greek New Testament vocabulary of some five thousand words, there are somewhat more than 25,000 meanings in all."[1] This averages out to five meanings for each word. The Hebrew language, because of its many homographs, has an even higher percentage.

Any doctrine of inspiration must give guidance when one encounters a biblical word that has more than one meaning. Which is the inspired meaning? Or are all of its meanings equally inspired? And how can one tell?

In any given context, the inspired meaning is that which the inspired writer had in his mind and the first reader would have understood.

## Inflections of Words
## Convey Meaning

A survey of statements about the inspiration of the Bible shows that they usually neglect, and sometimes even ignore, the significance of the meaning given a sentence by the *inflection* of a word—those prefixes, infixes, and suffixes added to the word that give further meaning to its stem (for example, *rekindled* and *kindled* have nuances that *kindle* doesn't have).[2]

Perhaps this is because the words in the English language have lost most of their inflections, so that all that are left are inflections such as "have," "had," and "having"; or "I," "me," and "my." So it wouldn't seem so important to call attention to a word's inflection; but the Greek verb has almost five hundred different inflections.

Therefore, an adequate definition of the inspiration of the Bible must take into account not only the stems of words but also their inflections. The "wording" of the Bible includes inflections.

## Meaning Found in the Sentence

Meaning lies in the sentence, not in the individual word. By *sentence* I mean a semantic sentence, which might also be a grammatical clause, even a phrase. Sometimes the sentence can be a single word, provided it can borrow meaning from its adjoining sentences, like the word *stop* when its surrounding sentences identify the persons who are to stop and what to stop and where.

Strictly speaking, words, by themselves, yield no meaning. The meanings that a dictionary attributes to a word are the ones the word is capable of contributing to a sentence provided the wording of that sentence is amenable to it. The meaning that word contributes to the sentence is under the strict regimen of its surrounding words. Only the combination of all the words in its syntactic context determines which of a word's dictionary meanings it brings to its sentence. You are never justified to choose a particular definition because it is theologically coherent.

## Language as a Part of Culture

An additional significant characteristic of language is that it is an essential part of culture (culture being nothing more than the characteristics of some people who have formed a group). People are fallen because they descend from Adam; no part of them escapes Adam's curse. So culture is fallen, all of it. So human language (not that of angels or any other unfallen creature) is fallen. It is not harsh of me, therefore, to call fallen human language limited and faulty. The Bible was written in this kind of human language!

Who knows for sure whether God created Adam with a language or whether Adam had to make one up? When one reads the story of Adam in the Bible, it looks like he was skillful in his language from the start. We will make this assumption.

And I suppose Eve also came equipped in the same way. But with Eve's arrival, culture came also. I am sure that at the beginning they had difficulty communicating, and I am also sure that it didn't take long for language to accommodate itself to the new culture.

Adam was not programmed with animal names. He made up a word for his wife and perhaps one for "fire." And I am sure that Adam or one of his descendants made up one for "refine" while a culture of metallurgy was being developed.

I think it safe to say—in fact my theology requires it—that this language, though limited to the intellectual capacity of the first pair, was not to be faulted. Neither was the burgeoning primordial culture. Only after the Fall did this culture, along with its language, begin to degenerate.

IMPLICATIONS FOR OUR UNDERSTANDING
OF INSPIRATION

This all too brief look at some of the basic characteristics of language suggests nevertheless some important implications for our understanding of the nature of inspiration. It may even require that some of our long-held notions about inspiration undergo correction.

### Both Symbol and Meaning Are Inspired

Language conveniently divides into two unequal parts: symbol and meaning. Symbol is the convention agreed upon by speaker and listener. The symbol begins as a sound one makes. It in turn can be symbolized by a squiggle one makes on a page. Then you have writing. These symbols carry the meaning from the speaker/writer to the listener/reader. Meaning is the cargo that symbols carry.

There can be no doubt that symbols exist solely for the purpose of conveying meaning. So meaning, by that much, is more important than symbol. Although facial expressions, posture, gesture, and intonation also are symbols, the major conveyance by far is verbal. The nonverbal communications are lost when the sound becomes a squiggle.

Each word is a boxcar; together they compose a train. The train is a sentence. The cargo is more important than the train, since the sole reason for the train's existence is to carry cargo.

Because of this, our understanding of inspiration should embrace the whole of the Bible's language, not just the Bible's symbols. If the language of the Bible is inspired, it is completely inspired in both its parts equally, symbol *and* meaning. This is not either/or inspiration but both/and—both symbol and meaning are inspired. And the inspiration of the meaning is more important than the inspiration of the symbol.

### The Importance of Verbal Inspiration

In my zeal to promote the inspiration of the *meaning* of the Scriptures and its priority over verbal inspiration, I may have created the impression that verbal inspiration is unimportant. Let me take some time to discuss just how important I believe verbal inspiration really is.

Let's think of a word as something like a section of a fence. You may have a goodly number of sections joined together like the old-fashioned drift fence of the West, which wagered it could outlast the patience of any cow. No matter how many sections you add, the fence refuses to define a field until the fence is closed. If you should choose to change the fence after you have closed it, you have changed by that much the definition of the field. The fence exists to protect the delineations of the field. It is but a means to an end. The more important thing is the field. The means is also important, however, for any change in it alters the field.

Let a single section represent a single word.

The fence sections are words. When the sections are closed, you have a sentence. The field within the fence is the thought that combination of words is designed to define. Change one word, you change the thought. So the United Nations translator must wait until the speaker closes the fence before he has any thought to translate.

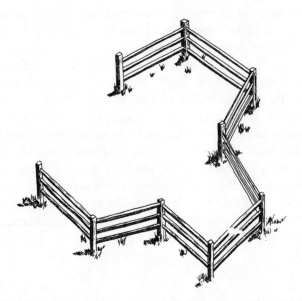

No matter how many sections, it does not define a field.

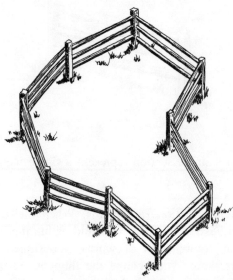

Only when the fence is closed does it define a field.

The field enclosed by the fence is a patchwork of beds and rows of beans and carrots and peas and corn and violets and roses and radishes and so on.

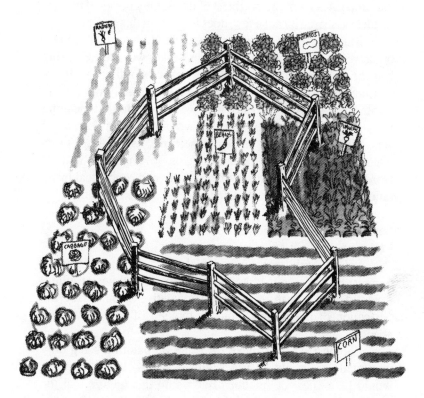

The contents of the field are determined by the shape and size of the fence. The words control the meaning of the sentence.

So what happens to the content of the field when a fence post is moved over a bit to one side or the other? The answer is clear. To the extent that the post is moved over, the field enclosed by the fence is altered. In the same way, the meaning of a sentence is altered when its wording is altered.

Often the change in wording does not change the meaning in any way that we can articulate or sometimes even notice. But the subliminal mind can be affected. Some argue that in some contexts the switch to a synonym has no effect even on the subconscious of the brightest of us. But my personal linguistic theory, shared by not a few, does not permit this exception.

But there is no reason why we should ever take it upon ourselves to make any change in the Bible's wording. God first had the meaning. Then he chose the exact wording to convey that meaning. What was written down was exactly the way he wanted it said. And the only way we can get to that meaning is by a careful examination of that wording. We have no other way. When the meaning is God's meaning, its wording is sacrosanct. It is because the meaning is so important that its wording is important. In our efforts to defend conceptual inspiration, we must not cease defending verbal inspiration.

## Some Thoughts on the Meaning of *Perfect*

We are quite ambiguous in the way we use the word *perfect*. Sometimes it is a relative term, sometimes absolute. I would like to use the term in a relative manner, for the perfection of the Bible should be thought of as relative, not absolute.

Should God ever make for us an oil painting using only man-made materials—brushes, oils, canvas—by definition it would be a "perfect" picture. But would this require that the detail in the picture exceed the detail that the limited number of nerve endings on our retina is able to distinguish? And under the scrutiny of the magnifying glass would the drawing of the cat's whisker be perfect even when perspective requires that the whisker's breadth be narrower than what the finest of man's brushes is capable of drawing? And would a "perfect" picture of that whisker show the varying shade on it caused by the light source?

And should God choose to do a watercolor of the same scene, would the painting be less perfect? When a person stands at a proper distance from a finely crafted painting, the leaves on the branches of a tree appear perfect in detail. But upon closer examination, those leaves are little more than green blobs.

Isn't it more reasonable to label "perfect" what a perfect artist is able to do with the human materials he must use?

Human languages—their grammar, their idioms, their vocabularies, and their definitions—were the material God chose to employ to communicate with us. And it is a perfect communication, but not as perfect as it would have been had he communicated the same message to angels in their language.

Whatever God does is perfect. When he created the animals, he created perfect ones. The elephant, the eagle, and man himself were each created with perfect vision. Yet Adam saw better than the elephant, and the eagle saw better than Adam. All three were perfect, not absolutely, but relatively— that is, relative to the niche they were created to occupy. Each had perfect vision for that niche.

The same is true with manufacturing tolerances. When the design engineer allows a certain tolerance for a certain part of a steam locomotive, say plus or minus .01 inches, any part made within that tolerance is perfect. That is, as far as the engineer knows, no part made within that tolerance will adversely affect the efficiency of the locomotive. On the other hand, a watch part has a tolerance of plus or minus .0001 inches. So what is perfect for a locomotive is not perfect for a watch.

## Some Thoughts about Precision[3]

While we are at it, a word or two should also be said about precision. In a culture such as ours, we highly respect the scientist and his way of doing things. Science is precise; therefore precision is a moral good and imprecision is an evil. The Bible is moral; therefore the Bible is precise. This is how we impose our own scientific culture on the Bible to produce a phantom Bible, one that is defined with theological precision but in reality does not exist.

Some well meaning Christian leaders have constructed a doctrine of the Bible from a purely theological base. What they have produced, I must admit, is beautiful and admirably cohesive; but it hardly describes the Bible that actually exists.

Carl Sagan of "Cosmos" fame reportedly said that the Bible cannot be God's word because it is not written in scientific language. (I won't get into a discussion about the arrogance of a novice propounding a theology of what God couldn't or wouldn't do, though I have to confess it would be fun.) Sagan echoes what apparently some theologians wish for so badly, that when they construct a theology of biblical inspiration, they can actually believe that the Bible is written in scientific language.

However, he who can't distinguish between $H_2O$ and water is unqualified to interpret the Bible. Science creates a language with discrete terms; the Bible was written in ordinary languages which had little need for such precision.

Some people seem to think it would be an improvement on the Bible if it sounded like an insurance policy. Even in its law genre, the Bible does not sound like our modern laws do.

How does one inflicted with this "scientific" nonsense exegete the word *about* (*hōsei*) in Acts 19:7, "There were about twelve men in all"? The only legitimate excuse for the use of this word here is to make fuzzy the edges of the word *twelve*. And if the Bible is inspired, its sentences are; and *hōsei* is just as inspired as any other word in that sentence.[4] And how, pray tell, would one exegete 1 Corinthians 1:14-16?

> I am thankful that I did not baptize any of you except Crispus and Gaius, so no one can say that you were baptized into my name. (Yes, I also baptized the household of Stephanas; beyond that, I don't remember if I baptized anyone else.)

There are altogether too many round numbers in the Bible to attribute it to a statistical curiosity. The precise counts of tribes and nations and armies would vary each day with births and deaths, enlistments and discharges. Round numbers are designed to be imprecise.

Every language without exception, the biblical languages included, has devised convenient conventions to introduce approximations, which occur not infrequently. A biblical doctrine of the Bible must accommodate comfortably these conventions. Whatever we do, let us describe what is really there.

The litmus test to all we say about the Bible is, "Are we describing what is actually there?"

## Some Thoughts about
## Inerrancy and Infallibility

*The Bible was written in a "fallen" language.* As I showed earlier, the logic is quite simple. Language and society are essential parts of man. When Adam sinned, all his descendants sinned with him. This is mankind's predicament and will remain until the time when those who have been redeemed will enjoy total regeneration.

Mankind is fallen, completely, in all its components, including the societies and languages it produces. God chose to employ three of these languages as the principal vehicles for his communication with man. The languages he used were intricately and inseparably a part of the men he chose (Moses, Paul, et al.) to write down his communication to man. He used *their* vocabularies, the meanings *they* put to those vocabularies, and *their* way with words. In all of this, we should expect each human author's contribution to differ from the rest.

We would expect fallen language to contain faulty taxonomies and definitions, ambiguities, and so on. At first notice, we are tempted to believe that God, to preserve his integrity, skirts around these inadequacies and employs a sort of pasteurized language. But this supposed solution fails to address the problem. For, upon further reflection, we recognize that the fallenness of a person's language is an accurate reflection of that person's fallenness. Any effort to purge the language would have no effect on that person's own faulty taxonomies, cloudy definitions, and ambiguities. Furthermore, we of the fallen race are, by our own fallenness, absolutely incapable of doing our own skirting around or improving of our language or even identifying where the language is faulted.

If our humanness is incapable of understanding a concept, then our language is incapable of writing about it. Whether or not God did any skirting would not affect our understanding of it.

Furthermore, it seems to me that our language's fallenness supplies part of its music. One can argue that there is something dishonest at the root of metaphor that is not found in simile. That is, it seems more truthful to say "he is like a bull in a china closet" than to say "he is a bull in a china closet." This may be so, but according to my taste, metaphor outranks simile. I get aesthetic pleasure out of presuming the nuances of *as* and *like*. By the same token, idioms, especially the multiworded ones, are equally dishonest. Yet they are musical notes in our language. I wouldn't want to deprive our language of them.

We don't know if what I have been talking about is true. I can only surmise. For my fallenness has excised my ability to detect where that fallenness has affected the language of the Bible.

I called language limited and faulty. I have some explaining to do. In other words, language is a slice of the pie called "culture"; of all its slices, it is perhaps the most characteristic of the whole pie. The most serious mistake we can make about a language is to fail to understand that it is indigenous to its culture as much or more so than any other part. One knows a language no better than one knows the culture that uses it.

*Inerrancy and infallibility are limited to the autographs*, the actual documents penned by Isaiah and Luke and the rest of the human authors of the Bible.[5] (Chapters 3 and 4 will demonstrate that since pollution has entered, the characteristics of inerrancy and infallibility cannot be attributed to copies of the Greek and Hebrew Testaments nor to translations of the Bible.) As far as we know, the autographs no longer exist; at least none has been found. And knowing our propensity to worship relics, perhaps it is better this way.

Defenders of a high view of inspiration are often criticized for devoting too much time defending and describing documents that no longer exist. But, as I have already said, the apologist can't pick his subject. Whether he likes it or not, he must defend what is being attacked.

Some introduce an ersatz distinction between *inerrant* and *infallible* and are thus able to espouse one and deny the other. My dictionary defines one of these words "free from error" and suggests the other word as a synonym to it. The other word is defined "incapable of error; unerring; sure; certain; incapable of error in defining doctrines touching faith or morals." I won't tell you which one was which because I want you to guess. I have to confess, I can't distinguish between the two. To me the Bible is either both or neither.

He who claims that the Bible is one and not the other places himself under the suspicion that he espouses a hidden agenda, an agenda he is too frightened to be candid about.

*Inerrancy and infallibility apply equally to every part of Scripture*. It is a gross misreading of the Bible to assume that we can divide it between being inerrant and infallible when it talks about doctrine and practice and being neither when it talks about nature and history.

The Bible has so integrated history and doctrine that they form the warp and woof of its fabric; it is impossible to form a judgment about one without doing the same with the other. When you separate redemption, love, and justice from crucifixion and resurrection, you wind up with only one reasonable position—neither can be believed. There can be no question that the Bible wants us to believe equally as much in both its history and its doctrine.

I do not like either *inerrant* or *infallible* because they are absolute words and, therefore, brook no qualification. Yet if I have to use them, honesty requires that I qualify them when I describe the nature of the biblical languages by recognizing that those languages, both in symbol and meaning, are less than absolutely perfect. For they are as ambiguous as other languages and contain "grammatical errors" which the definitive grammars disguise by using such terms as *anacoluthon* and *solecism*. Idioms are deformed grammar that we like so much we use them with pleasure.

I am more comfortable when I describe the Bible with the same words the Bible does: *pure*, *truth*, and *perfect* (1 Peter 2:2; John 17:17; Psalm 19:7). For we use these words more frequently in relative terms.

> Like newborn babies, crave pure spiritual milk, so
> that by it you may grow up in your salvation.
>
> (1 Peter 2:2)
>
> Sanctify them by the truth; your word is truth.
>
> (John 17:17)
>
> The law of the LORD is perfect,
>     reviving the soul.
> The statutes of the LORD are trustworthy,
>     making wise the simple.     (Psalm 19:7)

There is one absolute statement I would like to make about the Bible: What appeared on the pages of the autographs was exactly what God wanted and is to be believed, obeyed, and not tampered with!

And though the autographs were written in human languages that are, among other things, ambiguous and fallen, the stream—God's communication to man—flows through this section of the pipe as pure and perfect as its source is. Cause for the stream's pollution will not be found here, but in later sections that connect the fountainhead to the faucet—our mind, heart, and life.

The extent of this pollution we will now investigate.

Chapter 2, Notes

1. Jan de Waard and Eugene A. Nida, *From One Language to Another: Functional Equivalence in Bible Translating* (Nashville: Thomas Nelson Publishers, 1986), 144.

2. Actually, English inflections are more complicated than this. Sometimes the spelling of the word changes completely (for instance, *I* changes to *my* to indicate possession), and sometimes the spelling doesn't change at all (*read* is spelled the same whether you read this book tomorrow or you read it yesterday).

3. Cf. D. A. Carson, *Exegetical Fallacies* (Grand Rapids, Mich.: Baker Book House, 1984), 108.

4. Of the twenty-one times *hōsei*, usually translated by the English word *about*, appears in the New Testament, it appears eleven times to fuzz up numbers. Twice it appears in the phrase "about five thousand men" (Matthew 14:21; Luke 9:14) and once in each of the following phrases: "about twelve men" (Acts 19:7), "about thirty years old" (Luke 3:23), "about eight days" (Luke 9:28), "about the sixth hour" (Luke 23:44), "in groups of about fifty each" (Luke 9:14), "about an hour later" (Luke 22:59), "a group numbering about a hundred and twenty" (Acts 1:15), "about three thousand" (Acts 2:41), "at about three in the afternoon" (Acts 10:3). Wise people have learned to think with approximations. Some of us find the exercise repulsive. All of us should try to think with them. And *hōsei* is in no way the only means by which Greek expresses approximations.

5. This simple description of the autographs will do when referring to them. However, when debating their nature, it is inadequate. The book of Isaiah contains several prophecies proclaimed at different times under very different circumstances. We do not know whether or not Isaiah wrote each one down after preaching it; we certainly cannot forbid him from doing so. And if he did this, after they were all finished, but before they were published together as a single scroll, we would not be certain whether or not Isaiah (or whoever did it) employed some redaction or even editing when he joined them all together.

And as for Paul's Ephesians, we are reasonably certain that it was a circular letter written to the churches in the Roman province of Asia, where the most prominent church would be at Ephesus. Although the great majority of manuscripts include the word *Ephesus* in the salutation, the few oldest and best leave it out; but without another name to take its place, the Greek sentence doesn't make much sense. Omitting "in Ephesus" while retaining the participle "to be" reduces the sentence to a grossly unnatural, out of place, irrelevant, platonic observation about the ontological character of the epistle's recipients.

A very plausible explanation suggests that enough "original" copies were made to go around and that the name of each of the churches of Asia was inserted in that place. If such is the case, which one is the autograph? Furthermore, it is extremely difficult to identify the authors of multiauthor scrolls such as Psalms and Proverbs. One must read the article by George I. Mavrodes, "The Inspiration of Autographs," *Evangelical Quarterly* 41 (January-March 1969):19-29.

**Chapter 3**

# The Printed Greek New and Hebrew Old Testaments Are Inspired with Very Little Pollution

*T*hough the water is pure at the spring, every section of pipe connecting it to the faucet from which we drink has breeches that allow pollution to enter into the stream.

The first section of pipe is called "transmission." This is the history of the copies of the autographs, their discovery, editing, and collating. Furthermore, it includes the effort to reconstruct the autographs from these copies and the publishing of the reconstructed autographs in the printed Greek New and Hebrew Old Testaments now on sale at the bookstore.

Transmission spans the history of the Bible, which begins with the first copy of an autograph and continues on unremittingly into the present time and will continue on with no end in view until the end of the world.

It would be patently foolish to lay claim that these present-day, published Greek and Hebrew Testaments have no mistakes in them. But just how much pollution occurs in the transmission of the text? And do we have this intrusion under control? Are we making headway to reduce and ultimately to eliminate this source of pollution? Happily, we will discover in this chapter that the printed Greek New and Hebrew Old Testaments are surprisingly accurate.

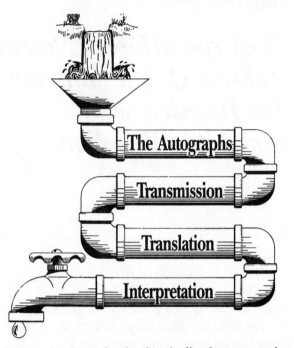

Communication—that is, the pipeline between spring and faucet—goes all the way from the mind and heart of God to the mind, heart, and life of man.

### THE MANUSCRIPTS THAT ARE KNOWN TO EXIST

Most Christians know that most of their Old Testament is a translation of manuscripts written in Hebrew and all of their New Testament in Greek. Only a few are aware that portions of Ezra (4:8-6:18; 7:12-26) and Daniel (2:4-7:28) and a single verse out of Jeremiah (10:11) were written originally in Aramaic, a sister language to Hebrew differing from it about as much as Norwegian differs from Swedish.

As I have already said, there is no autograph of a biblical scroll known to survive, and expectations that one might still surface are well nigh hopeless. The latest references I have been able to find that mention surviving autographs are in the writings of Peter of Alexandria (died 311 A.D.) and perhaps Tertullian (died ca. 215/20 A.D.).

> Now it was the preparation, about the third hour, as
> the accurate books have it, and the autograph copy
> itself of the Evangelist John, which up to this day has
> by divine grace been preserved in the most holy church
> of Ephesus, and is there adored by the faithful.[1]

> Come now, you who would indulge a better curiosity,
> if you would apply it to the business of your salvation,
> run over the apostolic churches, in which the very
> thrones of the apostles are still pre-eminent in their
> places, in which their own authentic writings are read,
> uttering the voice and representing the face of each
> of them severally. Achaia is very near you, (in which)
> you find Corinth. Since you are not far from
> Macedonia, you have Philippi; (and there too) you
> have the Thessalonians. Since you are able to cross
> to Asia, you get Ephesus. Since, moreover, you are
> close upon Italy, you have Rome, from which there
> comes even into our own hands the very authority (of
> apostles themselves).[2]

Tertullian's quote may refer to the autographs or the Greek originals
(rather than the Latin translations), or to the full unmutilated
copies as opposed to the garbled ones of the heretics.[3] Regardless,
the disappearance of the autographs is perhaps providential, for
God knows how we Christians tend to worship relics.[4]

Only manuscript copies survive (*manuscript* means "hand
copied"). Manuscripts were the only way of publishing until
the middle of the fifteenth century when Gutenberg invented
movable type. The earliest known New Testament manuscripts
are at least ten years removed from the autographs they copied.
The oldest manuscript we know of is the John Rylands fragment
$P^{52}$, five partial verses from the Gospel of John dated about
125 A.D. (see the illustration on the following page). This date,
plus or minus twenty-five years, was established by the famous
papyrologist Colin Henderson Roberts in 1935 and has re-
mained remarkably solid. However, Kurt and Barbara Aland
remark, "the consensus has come in recent years to regard 125

as representing the later limit, so that $P^{52}$ must have been copied *very soon* [italics mine] after the Gospel of John was itself written in the early 90s A.D."[5]

*The John Rylands fragment P*$^{52}$

And the oldest Old Testament manuscript is from Qumrân, a set of fragments from Leviticus, the script so old that you can't find a scholar who believes that it could be that old. Solomon A. Birnbaum ventures as far back as the fifth century B.C.[6] Many other scholars date the fragments in the fourth to third centuries B.C.[7]

People value ancient literature so highly that every surviving manuscript, even a manuscript fragment, is carefully edited, collated, published, and studied. There is a single exception to this rule: the Bible. The number is so great that this work has been done to only half the surviving manuscripts. Their number exceeds that of other literature of the same age by more than one hundred to one.

## Classical Scholars and
## New Testament Documents

A significant rift exists between the attitudes the classical historian and the New Testament radical critic have toward their documents. Trained classicists construct with far greater confidence their history of the first Christian century using far less reliable documentation than the radical critics who have far more and better documentation. The classical scholar A. N. Sherwin-White expresses his wonder about the historicity of the Book of Acts:

> For Acts the confirmation of historicity is overwhelming. Yet Acts is, in simple terms and judged externally, no less of a propaganda narrative than the Gospels, liable to similar distortions. But any attempt to reject its basic historicity even in matters of detail must now appear absurd. Roman historians have long taken it for granted.[8]

And the classicist turned biblical scholar F. F. Bruce expresses his bewilderment:

> It is a curious fact that historians have often been much readier to trust the New Testament records than have many theologians. Somehow or other, there are people who regard a 'sacred book' as *ipso facto* under suspicion, and demand much more corroborative evidence for such a work than they would for an ordinary secular or pagan writing. From the viewpoint of the historian, the same standards must be applied to both.[9]

Bruce goes on to describe the differences in data between classical history and New Testament history both in quantity and quality:

> There are in existence over 5,000 Greek manuscripts of the New Testament in whole or in part. The best and most important of these go back to somewhere about AD 350, the two most important being the Codex Vaticanus . . . and the well-known Codex Sinaiticus. . . .
>
> Perhaps we can appreciate how wealthy the New Testament is in manuscript attestation if we compare the

textual material for other ancient historical works. For Caesar's *Gallic War* (composed between 58 and 50 BC) there are several extant MSS, but only nine or ten are good, and the oldest is some 900 years later than Caesar's day. Of the 142 books of the Roman History of Livy (59 BC-AD 17) only thirty-five survive; these are known to us from not more than twenty MSS of any consequence, only one of which, and that containing fragments of Books iii-vi, is as old as the fourth century. Of the fourteen books of the *Histories* of Tacitus (*c*. AD 100) only four and a half survive; of the sixteen books of his *Annals*, ten survive in full and two in part. The text of these extant portions of his two great historical works depends entirely on two MSS, one of the ninth century and one of the eleventh. The extant MSS of his minor works (*Dialogus de Oratoribus*, *Agricola*, *Germania*) all descend from a codex of the tenth century. The History of Thucydides (*c*. 460-400 BC) is known to us from eight MSS, the earliest belonging to *c*. AD 900, and a few papyrus scraps, belonging to about the beginning of the Christian era. The same is true of the History of Herodotus (*c*. 488-428 BC). Yet no classical scholar would listen to an argument that the authenticity of Herodotus or Thucydides is in doubt because the earliest MSS of their works which are of any use to us are over 1,300 years later than the originals.[10]

Bible scholars boast of the New Testament that there are over five thousand Greek manuscripts, six thousand Latin, and one thousand in other versions which we know to have survived. How many more are yet to be discovered is anybody's guess.

### The Manuscripts Differ between Themselves

Yet we must be honest and acknowledge that not all these manuscripts are exactly alike. There are differences between them.

This should not surprise us once we understand the process by which copies were made.

A scribe would have a copy, an exemplar, before him and, with his eyes flitting back and forth, would produce a new copy. Or a number of scribes would listen while the exemplar was read aloud, and all the scribes would write down what they heard[11]—a sort of book factory, if you please.

If the book was important, it would be proofread—sometimes a number of times. Corrections would be entered usually between the lines or in the margin. The magnificent fourth century manuscript Codex Sinaiticus demonstrates its importance by the fact that it had more than eight proofreaders.

I am talking about professional scribes here. We have every reason to believe that the first generation of the brand new church was composed almost completely of the lower class and slaves and could not afford the professional scribe. Instead, those who could read and write produced copies of the sacred text with little or no proofreading.

During that first generation of Christians, expectation for the soon return of Christ ran high. The letters and gospels and copies thereof would make do as surrogates of the absent author to this burgeoning church too large now to be served in person by the apostles. About the time the church had to realize that it must prepare for the long haul and when heresies were producing competing Bibles, the emperor Constantine (ca. 274/80-337 A.D.) was converted to Christianity. He brought the church out of the underground and gave it enough prosperity so that it could afford professional scribes who carefully copied and whose copies were carefully proofread.

Almost all the manuscripts we know to exist come from this period which extends from Constantine all the way to Gutenberg. A few papyri, mostly in fragments, survive from the earlier period and are carefully studied and published by scholars.

### THE IMPORTANT ROLE OF THE TEXUAL CRITIC

It is humanly impossible for one to copy off a whole Bible by hand and not make a mistake. None of these five-thousand-plus Greek manuscripts agrees precisely with any other. Which is the correct one? Or better, how can we reconstruct an autograph by comparing these faulty surviving manuscripts? The person who works at this is called a *textual critic*, and this kind of study is called *textual criticism* (or *lower criticism*, not to be confused with *higher criticism*).

Liberal and conservative Bible scholars are sharply divided in their higher criticism techniques and conclusions, but there is no such conflict when it comes to textual criticism.[12] Both use the same Hebrew and Greek Testaments, along with their footnotes of variant readings. Both apply to them the same principles of textual criticism and reach the same conclusions.

Although the principles are identical for both the Hebrew Old Testament and the Greek New Testament, their manuscript histories differ so much that each must be described separately. Old Testament scribes deliberately destroyed manuscripts but made an effort to build a textual apparatus which contained, among other items, variant readings and various word counts designed to ensure accurate copying. On the other hand, copyists of the New Testament did not destroy manuscripts but kept no record of variants. What results is a scarcity of Hebrew manuscripts—most of which have an elaborate set of footnotes—and an abundance of Greek New Testament manuscripts with no footnotes—most of which show corrections, many in more than one style of handwriting.

### How the Textual Critic Works

Before we look over his shoulder and watch the textual critic at work, let's look at a couple of methods that at first thought one might think proper but which the textual critic would never use.

One might think at first that the job would be easy; simply take a vote and go with the majority. But that doesn't work. Too many things can happen to affect the volume of production. It is no coincidence that most Greek manuscripts come from Byzantium and most Latin versions in manuscript form from Western Europe. This is because all the other Christian centers fell to Islam early, but Byzantium fell late and Western Europe, except Spain, never fell.[13] Neither is it a coincidence that practically all of the earliest manuscripts are from Egypt, for that is the only civilization center where the climate inhibits their decay.

Nor should the textual critic go by the age of the manuscript alone as if the older would always be the better, for we don't know how old the parent manuscript was when its offspring was born. A seventh century manuscript might have been copied from a sixth century manuscript, but a fifteenth century manuscript might have been copied from a third century manuscript.

Now, let's look over the shoulder of the textual critic and watch him at work. *First*, he studies and evaluates the individual manuscript, editing it, collating it, dating it, and, if possible, discovering where it was written down.

*Second*, he compares the patterns of its variant wordings. A variant wording is a wording differing from other manuscripts. He seeks from this comparison to identify the manuscript he is studying with some group of manuscripts which has the same patterns of variant wordings. There are now five of these groups of New Testament manuscripts commonly accepted by the textual critics, each with a geographical name: Western European, Western African, Byzantine, Caesarean, and Alexandrian.[14] There are now three families of Old Testament manuscripts, the Masoretic Text, the Samaritan Pentateuch, and the Septuagint, whose geographical locations are tentatively located at Babylon, Israel, and Egypt respectively.

The idea of sorting out manuscripts by affinity groups and locating the groups geographically seems logical. However, the hard realities of history frustrate the textual critic as he tries to do this. He conceives of the first manuscript arriving at Byzantium, which, of course, would contain its share of mistakes. Copies of this manuscript would be made at Byzantium, each containing a family likeness because they all would contain the mistakes of their parent manuscript plus, of course, a few new ones differing from the old ones copied off the parent manuscript.

All this is fine and good and plays right into the hands of the textual critic. The problem is, however, how are you to keep Byzantium sealed off from other sources? How can you keep another copy of the Bible from arriving at Byzantium? And what do you do with the copy a scribe made from both of these manuscripts in which he used his own uncritical judgment as to which of the two he would use in any given text and yet does not indicate which copy it was?

This kind of event happened not rarely. It was done by the copyists, who were forced into the textual criticism mode by circumstances beyond their control. In textual criticism's parthenogenetic monastery, sex is sin. Until this knot can be untied, the whole structure of the genealogical method is at risk.

*Third*, by the use of commonly accepted rules of textual criticism, the textual critic seeks to produce the common parent of each group of manuscripts which share the same patterns of variant wordings. The commonly accepted rules are: Other things being equal,

1. Because manuscripts have the tendency to grow, the shorter variant is to be preferred.
2. Because copyists have the tendency to smooth out the more awkward wording, the more difficult variant is to be preferred.
3. That variant which most easily accounts for how the alternate variant could have occurred is to be preferred.
4. That alternate which best represents the style and vocabulary of the author and the running thought of the context of the verse is to be preferred.

*Fourth*, by using these same rules, the textual critic reconstructs from the common parents of these groups the original autographs.

Textual critics have completed none of these four steps. And they have done so poorly on the second step that many contemporary critics despair of ever getting it done. And neither the ancient copyist nor the modern textual critic wears a prophet's mantle.

## How Much Do Textual Critics Agree?

Within the last century, efforts to create the New Testament autographs, though made independently, are surprisingly similar, so much so that it gives one confidence that textual critics are on the right track. Brooke Foss Westcott and Fenton John Anthony Hort, in 1881, employing external evidence almost exclusively, and Bernard Weiss, in 1900, employing internal evidence almost exclusively, produced surprisingly similar Greek New Testaments.

Even though New Testament textual critics are poles apart when it comes to their confidence in the trustworthiness of the autographs, their consensus on the actual wording of the text is not broken; liberal and conservative are agreed. And there is even greater agreement over the present condition of the Old Testament text than over the text of the New.

## How Badly Are the Greek and Hebrew Testaments Polluted?

*The text of the New Testament.* For the Greek New Testament, the most generally accepted figure for significant pollution at this section of pipe is one-tenth of 1 percent.[15] That is, if all the uncertain words were assembled in a five hundred page Greek Testament, they would occupy only four-tenths of a single page. The state of the text of the Greek New Testament is purer than Ivory Soap's 99 and 44/100 percent! Further, progress is continually being made in reducing this figure. We may confidently say that we have our arms around the problem, and these intrusive pollutants are under control.

Such a minuscule percentage is possible only if the ending of Mark (16:9-20) and the passage about the woman taken in adultery (John 7:53-8:11) are judged not to be part of the autographs, for each one is about six-tenths of a single page of a five hundred page Greek New Testament. Though both the United

Bible Society's Greek New Testament (the Greek Testament you find in the bookstore) and the Nestle-Aland Greek Testament include these two passages, they are set off by brackets, indicating words that were not in the autographs. A survey of the more popular modern English translations will reveal the uneasiness about these two texts, even outright rejection on the part of some.

And what are the prospects to further reduce the pollution entering the stream from this section of pipe? Experience allows us but one answer: There likely remain still buried in ruins or forgotten in some monastery corner manuscripts as old and older than we now have. And, with the aid of the computer, the techniques of textual criticism are bound to be refined to reduce that already small percentage of possible errors even more.

No such claim could have been made a hundred and fifty years ago. The standard Greek New Testament of that day was already three hundred years old. It was edited by the great Erasmus, Mr. Renaissance himself, who took some time out of nine months of his busy life to produce a copy for the newly established movable-type printing press. To do this, he went to Basel, Switzerland, where he found in its libraries a half-dozen Greek New Testament manuscripts, all recent. He was so ashamed of the quality of his work that he characterized it as "done headlong rather than edited."[16] Because of a publisher's blurb in the publisher Elzevir's second edition of Erasmus, Erasmus's Greek New Testament came to be known as "the Received Text."[17] This "Received Text" (Latin, *Textus Receptus*) was the standard, almost sole printed Greek text from the sixteenth century through the nineteenth century. It embraces the various editions of Erasmus, which very closely resemble each other, and was the basic text used by the translators of the King James Version.[18]

During the past hundred and fifty years, using not a half-dozen later, but rather hundreds of early manuscripts; not part of nine months, but years of study; not one person, but dozens have brought the printed Greek text to its present state of excellence.

The contrast between Erasmus's Greek Testament and the present standard Greek New Testament, especially when exaggerated by controversy, gives off a feeling of uncertainty about the degree of pollution now entering the stream at this section of pipe. Yet the overwhelming majority of those whose academic production lies in this field of endeavor endorse the present standard Greek New Testament, far outweighing both in quantity and quality the minutiae who tenaciously still espouse the work of Erasmus, and who bring to the defense of their loyalty no better argument than the providence of God. It would be just as logical to argue the merits of Adolf Hitler on the basis that he too put in his appearance within the providence of God.

*The text of the Old Testament.* The state of the art of Old Testament textual criticism is about two hundred years behind that of the New. Before the discovery of the Dead Sea Scrolls in 1947, the earliest sizable portions of the Hebrew Bible were dated at the tenth century A.D., for example the Aleppo and the Leningrad manuscripts. There are only a few of them.

The pages of these manuscripts were framed with the Masorah, a nondescript border of annotations on the text compiled by the Masoretes around 500-900 A.D. The Masorah includes elaborate word counts, diverse computations; memory gimmicks, and variant readings. The Masoretes regarded the text proper so sacrosanct that even when they concluded that a word was an intrusion or that a word had been changed, they left the text as is and entered these corrections in the Masorah. Additionally, they thought that by counting words and by identifying the middle word and letter in a book, they were guaranteeing its absolute accuracy. This guarantee required that careful attention be given to the Masorah, which the surviving manuscripts amply testify was not done.

This work was not done by a single Masoretic school, but by several whose Masorah differed. One manuscript exists from one school which is framed by a Masorah from another. The middle word in the Masorah more often than not is not the actual middle word in the text. And a manuscript exists where this Masorah has so lost its meaning that it has degenerated to mere indecipherable decoration!

Defenders of inspiration had to face the one-thousand-plus year hiatus between the time of the autographs and the date of the earliest surviving manuscripts. They had no other option than to depend on the Jewish attitudes toward the sacrosanct text, as reflected in the Talmud, to carry the text through these one-thousand-plus years in a near perfect transmission.

The discovery of the Dead Sea Scrolls surprised everybody. What was generally thought to be a hopeless impossibility actually occurred. Every book in the Old Testament save one is represented at least in a fragment by manuscripts written *before Christ*. The one-thousand-plus years have been bridged in a most remarkable way. Furthermore, the differences in the texts of the Dead Sea Scrolls and the tenth century ones are surprisingly slight. One manuscript, 1QIsa$^b$, is called by W. F. Albright "virtually identical" to the Masoretic Text.[19]

We must be warned that the Dead Sea Scrolls are what survives of a library of a Jewish sect which had deliberately separated itself from and had repudiated the mainstream of Judaism together with its scholarship. The prudent person can only predict that the sacred texts of the Old Testament held in the temple at Jerusalem reflected a more accurate copy of the autographs than those at Qumrân did. The slender evidence relating to the temple scrolls supports this. The only records we have imply that there were only four variants between the three copies in the temple and only thirty-two between the temple scroll that was taken by Vespasian to Rome and the Masoretic Text.[20]

Unlike the New Testament families where one text doesn't dominate the other texts so severely, among the three Old Testament families of manuscripts, the Masoretic greatly dominates the Septuagint and the Samaritan Pentateuch.

Other sources contribute somewhat to our efforts to recreate the autographs: the Targums (Aramaic paraphrases of the Bible); the Talmud (the authoritative body of Jewish tradition); the Syriac, Latin, Coptic, and Ethiopic versions; tertiary spin-offs from the Latin and Syriac. Yet when it comes to a single word, and often a phrase, a translation, even the Septuagint, is a poor witness to a variant, for we can't tell whether or not an idiom or a synonym is being used.

So what can I say about the amount of corruption infiltrating into the transmission section of the Old Testament pipe? Scholars have not been as ready to commit themselves to a percentage like the New Testament one-tenth of 1 percent. I don't think it would be much higher, but I am only presuming. We can say dogmatically, however, that the actual meaning of the Old Testament survives in its purity much better than human perception is able to notice.

And what of the future of Old Testament textual criticism? It is even brighter than that of the New. The possibility of finding more new manuscripts of the Old Testament than of the New is greater. And the refining of our printed Hebrew Old Testament is almost guaranteed to occur. The percentage of places in the Old Testament where pollution is possibly occurring is bound to be significantly reduced.

## COPIES OF THE ORIGINAL MANUSCRIPTS ARE INSPIRED

Can we say that a Greek New Testament that contains scribal errors and is, therefore, not an absolutely accurate reproduction of the autographs still is inspired? Yes, if our doctrine of inspiration is not theological but biblical; for the Bible itself clearly infers that copies of the autographs are also inspired.

The principal categorical biblical statements about its inspiration are 2 Peter 1:21, which says that the prophets were carried along by the Holy Spirit, and 2 Timothy 3:16-17, which states the purpose of the Bible. But in stating its purpose, it justifies its ability to accomplish this purpose by observing that it is inspired by God.

"Inspired by God" translates a single Greek word, *theopneustos*, which appears only once in the New Testament and here for the first time in all of Greek.[21] Did Paul invent a word which puzzled Timothy? Clearly, the Greek word means "inspired by God." The word *Scripture* in this verse translates the Greek word *graphē*. *Graphē* appears fifty times in the Greek New

Testament, and in every instance it means "Scripture," particularly, "Old Testament Scripture."

Do we have hard evidence that copies of the Old Testament autographs were called "Scripture" (*graphē*) in the New Testament? A search of the fifty appearances of *graphē* in the New Testament reveals that Jesus read from the Scripture (*graphē*) in the synagogue at Nazareth (Luke 4:21) and Paul from the Scripture (*graphē*) in the synagogue at Thessalonica (Acts 17:2). The Ethiopian eunuch riding in his chariot on his way home from Jerusalem was reading a portion of Scripture (*graphē*, Acts 8:32-33). These were not autographs; they were copies. And copies contain scribal errors. Yet the Bible calls them *graphē*, and every *graphē* is inspired (2 Timothy 3:16). Yes, copies of the autographs are inspired.

Pollution entering at the section of pipe known as transmission is minor and is diminishing as the art of textual criticism continues to increase the accuracy of the text. We have our arms around the problem.

---

Chapter 3, Notes

1. Alexander Roberts et al., eds., *The Ante-Nicene Fathers: Translations of the Writings of the Fathers down to A.D. 325*, rev. A. Cleveland Coxe, American and auth. ed., 10 vols. (New York: The Christian Literature Co., 1885-87; reprint ed., Grand Rapids, Mich.: Wm. B. Eerdmans Publishing Co., 1956-57), vol. 6: *Fathers of the Third Century: Gregory Thaumaturgus, Dionysius the Great, Julius Africanus, Anatolius and Minor Writers, Methodius, Arnobius*, arrang. by A. Cleveland Coxe, 283.

2. Roberts et al., vol. 3: *Latin Christianity: Its Founder, Tertullian*, arrang. by A. Cleveland Coxe, 260.

3. Ibid.

4. Apparently the Christians were very near, if not there, to worshiping an autograph if Peter of Alexandria could say of the Ephesians about the Gospel of John that it "is there adored by the faithful."

5. Kurt Aland and Barbara Aland, *The Text of the New Testament: An Introduction to the Critical Editions and to the Theory and Practice of Modern Textual Criticism*, trans. Erroll F. Rhodes (Grand Rapids, Mich.: Wm. B. Eerdmans Publishing Co., 1987; Leiden: E. J. Brill, 1987), 85.

6. Charles F. Pfeiffer, *The Dead Sea Scrolls and the Bible*, Baker Studies in Biblical Archaeology (Grand Rapids, Mich.: Baker Book House, 1969), 29.

7. George Arthur Buttrick and Keith Crim, eds., *The Interpreter's Dictionary of the Bible*, 5 vols. (Nashville: Abingdon Press, 1962, 1976), 4:582-83, 1:795; William Sanford LaSor, "The Dead Sea Scrolls," in *The Expositor's Bible Commentary*, ed. Frank E. Gaebelein, 12 vols. (Grand Rapids, Mich.: Zondervan Publishing House, 1979), 1:397; Pfeiffer, 30.

8. A. N. Sherwin-White, *Roman Society and Roman Law in the New Testament* (Oxford: At the Clarendon Press, 1963), 189.

9. F. F. Bruce, *The New Testament Documents: Are They Reliable?*, 5th rev. ed. (Leicester, England: Inter-Varsity Press, 1984; Grand Rapids, Mich.: Wm. B. Eerdmans Publishing Co., 1984), 15.

10. Ibid., 16-17.

11. Documentary evidence that this actually happened is mysteriously missing. However, a number of manuscripts contain errors that could only occur because the scribe did not hear correctly when the exemplar was read aloud, errors which would not have been made if the scribe was looking at the exemplar.

12. I don't want to ignore a small group of biblical students, conservative to a man, who object violently to the direction the discipline has gone and who insist that we go back in time four hundred years to the first printed Greek text, that of Erasmus, the Roman Catholic scholar of the Renaissance. But their position is hardly one of an alternative principle of textual criticism, but rather one of none at all.

13. It is safe to assume that Christian publication centered around the Christian centers, especially the academic centers. So they would also be the centers for Bible production. In the period from the end of the apostolic age throughout the first millennium, academic centers developed probably in this order: in Jerusalem, Caesarea, Antioch, Alexandria, Carthage, Byzantium, and Rome. These would be equally active in the production of Bibles, and any difference in manuscript survival would be attributable more to climatic conditions than anything else.

However, an important historical reality enters the picture. With but one exception, Islam overran every one of these centers: first Jerusalem, 637 A.D.; then Caesarea, 638 A.D.; then Antioch, 638 A.D.; then Alexandria, 640 A.D.; then Carthage, 698 A.D.; then, about seven hundred years later, Byzantium, 1453 A.D. The only surviving one was Rome.

From 700 A.D. on, the only places where we would expect a lot of production would be from Europe and those areas that were not overrun by Islam. Christianity was snuffed out in many places and, in the others, just barely survived so that academic activity and book production, including Bibles, ground to a halt. This is enough from history to account for the fact that so many of our extant manuscripts come from the Byzantine-type Greek New Testament and the Latin Vulgate.

14. When I said "commonly accepted," I did not mean universally accepted. Kurt and Barbara Aland are notable exceptions (cf. Aland and Aland, 54-55, 66-67).

15. Cf. Brooke Foss Westcott and Fenton John Anthony Hort, *The New Testament in the Original Greek*, rev. American ed., 2 vols. (New York: Harper & Bros. Publishers, 1887, 1882), 2:2:

If the principles followed in the present edition are sound, this area may be very greatly reduced. Recognising to the full the duty of abstinence from peremptory decision in cases where the evidence leaves the judgement in suspense between two or more readings, we find that, setting aside differences of orthography, the words in our opinion still subject to doubt only make up about one sixtieth of the whole New Testament. In this second estimate the proportion of comparatively trivial variations is beyond measure larger than in the former; so that the amount of what can in any sense be called substantial variation is but a small fraction of the whole residuary variation, and can hardly form more than a thousandth part of the entire text.

16. Cf. Caspar Rene Gregory, *Canon and Text of the New Testament*, The International Theological Library (New York: Charles Scribner's Sons, 1912), 441; Bruce M. Metzger, *The Text of the New Testament: Its Transmission, Corruption, and Restoration*, 2d ed. (New York: Oxford University Press, 1968), 99; Frederick Henry Ambrose Scrivener, *A Plain Introduction to the Criticism of the New Testament for the Use of Biblical Students*, 4th ed., ed. Edward Miller, 2 vols. (London: George Bell & Sons, 1894), 2:183.

17. The same kind of thing happens today when a publisher makes a strong statement about the quality of one of its works, hoping that you will buy its book instead of its competitor's.

18. Actually, the designation *Textus Receptus* didn't arise until 1633, twenty-two years too late to be used by the translators of the King James Version.

19. W. F. Albright, "New Light on Early Recensions of the Hebrew Bible," in *Qumrân and the History of the Biblical Text*, ed. Frank Moore Cross and Shemaryahu Talmon (Cambridge: Harvard University Press, 1975), 143.

20. Christian D. Ginsburg, *Introduction to the Massoretico-Critical Edition of the Hebrew Bible*, with a Prolegomenon by Harry M. Orlinsky (New York: Ktav Publishing House Inc., 1966), 408, 410-11.

21. "It is strange that the earliest patristic use [of *theopneustos*] is as late as the third century, appearing about four times in Origin and once in Clement of Alexandria. The fourth century yields eight Christian authors (cited by Lampe) who also used *theopneustos*. By contrast during the second century several heathen writers used the word: Plutarch, Vettius Vallens, and the author of *Pseudo-Phocylides*, who possibly was a Jew or a Christian and who possibly also wrote the fifth book of the *Sibylline Oracles*. If Paul coined the word, it is squeezing it to find the word on heathen lips after so brief an interval. But it is possible." Edward W. Goodrick, "Let's Put 2 Timothy 3:16 Back in the Bible," *Journal of the Evangelical Theological Society* (December 1982): 483-84.

## RECOMMENDED READING

Greenlee, J. Harold. *Scribes, Scrolls, and Scripture: A Student's Guide to New Testament Textual Criticism*. Grand Rapids, Mich.: Wm. B. Eerdmans Publishing Co., 1985.

Klein, Ralph W. *Textual Criticism of the Old Testament: The Septuagint After Qumran*. Philadelphia: Fortress Press, 1974.

Wurthwein, Ernst. *The Text of the Old Testament: An Introduction to the Biblia Hebraica*. Translated by Erroll F. Rhodes. Grand Rapids, Mich.: Wm. B. Eerdmans Publishing Co., 1979.

Metzger, Bruce M. *The Text of the New Testament: Its Transmission, Corruption, and Restoration*. 2d ed. New York: Oxford University Press, 1968.

Ginsburg, Christian D. *Introduction to the Massoretico-Critical Edition of the Hebrew Bible*. Prolegomenon by Harry M. Orlinsky. Reprint ed. New York: Ktav Publishing House Inc., 1966.

Waltke, Bruce K. "The Textual Criticism of the Old Testament." In *The Expositor's Bible Commentary*, 1:209-28. Edited by Frank E. Gaebelein. 12 vols. Grand Rapids, Mich.: Zondervan Publishing House, 1979.

**Chapter 4**

# *Your Bible Is Inspired with Very Little Pollution*

*I*nspiration is that event when God communicates with man. The inspiration event that produced the Bible can be described as that event when the prophet/apostle spoke/wrote what the Holy Spirit revealed to him so that man may be illuminated and, thus, informed, moved, and motivated.

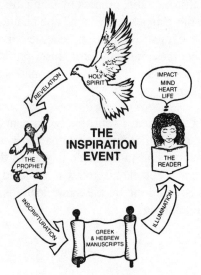

But few among us can read Greek and Hebrew and Aramaic, the languages God chose to communicate with man. Most of us must depend on translations of those languages into our own. How can I be confident that the translation I read is likewise the inspired word of God?

## THE NATURE OF TRANSLATION

### What Is Translation?

You have translation when the effect on the reader of a wording in language "A" is communicated by the use of the wording of language "B" to the reader of language "B." The translator, understanding the effect of a wording in the source language, constructs wording in the receptor language which conveys the same effect.

One can illustrate this process by using the same diagram that illustrates the "Inspiration Event" and changing the names of some of the figures. Revelation becomes divine guidance, the prophet becomes the translator, inscripturation becomes translation, and the Greek and Hebrew manuscripts become the translated Bible.

From here on, there is absolutely no change. For when there is good translation, its reader is impacted by the translation in the same manner and to the same degree as the first reader of the autograph. That is, his mind is affected by the same information, his emotions by the same feelings, and his will by the same motivation.

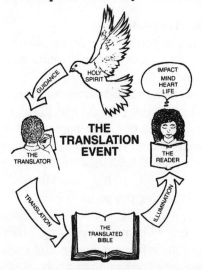

Joining these two diagrams illustrates how inspiration and translation relate. We place the translation diagram beside the inspiration diagram in such a manner that the *translator* takes the *reader's* place in the first diagram. It is almost like a double play: prophet to translator to reader. It has this significant difference, however: the ball thrown in the second part of the double play is a different kind of ball; the middle player has to juggle two kinds of balls, catching a baseball and throwing a football. That is, he must understand well the source language and use well the receptor language.

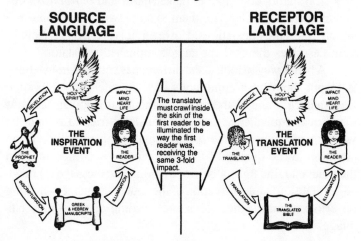

## What Is a Good Translation?

A translation is good to the degree that it produces the same knowledge, emotion, and motivation that the original language produced in the original reader.

I am not so sure our translators have given these three objectives equal attention. I would like to see a survey taken among the translators of our more popular Bibles that would inquire how much time they gave to each of the three. To ask the academic to evaluate the balance is foolish, for he is prejudiced toward knowledge. To him, knowledge is the most important thing that can happen to us.

Our culture, which has invented such pejorative terms as "rabble-rouser" and "inflammatory writing," hardly is in a position to compare the relative importance of emotion, motivation, and knowledge. "Wake up, be godly, stop your wickedness; for some don't know God. You are a disgrace!" (1 Corinthians 15:34, my own translation) is inflammatory.

In fact, the prophets were mainly rabble-rousers and their prophecy was inflammatory. I wonder what a translation would look like if its translators would pay attention to motivation and emotion. But the translator's unconscious revulsion to such writing makes him tone down such ungentlemanly expressions.

## Literal Translation versus Paraphrase

Translators don't like to make *literal* and *paraphrase* disjunctive terms and then use them to label two pigeonholes into which to sort the translations. However, it is often done. Neither term describes the goal for an accomplished translator.

A better way to look at the differences between translations is to put them on a continuous line. At one end is "Formal Equivalence," and at the other, "Functional Equivalence." At the formal equivalence end, the translator tries to mimic the wording and words of the source language, paying little or no attention to the quality of the sentences he is composing. On the other end, the translator tries to mimic the message—knowledge, emotion, and motivation of the source language—making no effort to match the words and wording of the source language.

**FORMAL
EQUIVALENCE**                                    **FUNCTIONAL
EQUIVALENCE**

---

Translations are spread out along this line from one extreme to the other depending upon the interests of the translators. This spectrum must *not* be thought of as illustrating the difference between "literal" and "paraphrase."

To maintain both objectives requires a gymnastic contortion impossible for one's literary anatomy. One objective must be sacrificed to the other; and any attention, howsoever brief, paid to one by so much damages the other.

It is impossible to translate the Bible word for word. A literal, one-on-one translation of John 3:16 would not be English. See for yourself: "Thus for he-loved the God the world that the son the only-born he-gave that every the believing into him not he-might-perish but he-might-have life eternal."

A paraphrase is the use of a number of words to translate a single word. "Is given by the inspiration of God" is a paraphrase of a single Greek word (*theopneustos*, 2 Timothy 3:16). But to introduce paraphrase when it is not the best way to translate an idea is ridiculous.

The skilled translator, keeping in mind that his goal is to affect the readers in the same way that the first readers were affected, discovers that his translation sometimes is word for word and sometimes paraphrastic (he couldn't care less which). This always happens when the translation is in good, idiomatic English, such as the Authorized Version. You can hardly find a sentence in it that does not contain at least some paraphrase. In fact, this is one of the causes, if not the chief cause, for the multi-centuried popularity of the Authorized Version.

A good translation emulates the character of the source language. For the New Testament, God selected a vernacular language, a language of the street and market place, a language of Semitic people who laced their Greek dialect with the idioms and wordings of their mother tongue.

To the first readers, Paul sounded far more like Ernest Hemingway sounds to us than like Shakespeare, who, by the way, wrote in the vernacular of his day. So a good translation today should sound more like Hemingway than like Shakespeare.

In a few circles—not the best informed—a debate continues about the relative value between *dynamic equivalence* and *formal equivalence* when translating. This debate is of sufficient size that a book of this nature must not ignore it.

By dynamic equivalence is meant what I have here espoused.[1] By formal equivalence is meant a verbal equivalence between the source and receptor languages as much as is possible and still make sense. Emotion and motivation as well as ease in reading are to be sacrificed to verbal equivalence.

Formal equivalence espousers have cut my *reductio ad absurdum* argument (my example of a literal translation of John 3:16) off at the pass by laying on the condition that as important as word for word translation is, it must not be done so consistently as to reduce the receptor's wording to nonsense.

However, such nonsense as "gird up the loins of your mind," one Semitic idiom overlaying another, is tolerated and excused with the observation that it is the preacher's job to "explain it," or, "It should be explained in the margin." To translate this nonsensical double idiom by the simple English idiom "pay attention" is deemed wrong because it does not translate the Greek word for word.

Devotees of formal equivalence, before they will be taken seriously by students of translation, must spell out in detail how much emotion and motivation, ease in reading, and meaning itself they are prepared to sacrifice in exchange for how much formal equivalence they gain. Further, they must produce actual examples in which all four of these elements are found and articulate how each element is affected. Where formal equivalence is found to diminish these elements, its proponents must argue persuasively why formal equivalence is important enough to accept such a loss.

Formal equivalence has failed to learn the lesson taught us by the very first effort to translate the Bible into English. It was attempted by John Wycliffe and his men in the 1300s. Their first effort was an "extremely literal and almost unreadable"[2] translation which didn't fly very well. It was revised to a more idiomatic English and became very popular.

The reverse was also attempted. The functional equivalent King James Version was revised in 1881 into a more formal equivalent version which never took off, to say nothing of replacing the ever-popular KJV.[3]

I have the firm conviction that the cause of formal equivalence is driven by a hidden agenda which I will seek to expose later on in this chapter.

### Translation Contributes to Pollution

But, sad to say, the translator is doomed to failure—"The translator is a traitor" translates the Italian proverb " *traduttore traditore*"—for he never completely tells the truth. Something always gets lost in the translation, and something foreign to the original will put in its appearance on the page of the translation. These are called *translation loss* and *translation distortion* and are not the fault of the translator. They are indigenous to the very nature of language itself. They are pollutants intruding at the translation section of the pipe that, therefore, cannot be completely stopped.

The problem is that these pollutants are difficult to detect, even impossible for anyone not at home in both languages. And even with this qualification, one must be linguistically alert and sensitive.

Significant losses and distortions can be corrected by good commentaries, and the problem can be leapfrogged by a proficiency in the source languages so that one is not dependent upon a translation. However, to feel at home in a dead language is well nigh impossible—some would say it is impossible.

### IS A TRANSLATION OF THE BIBLE INSPIRED?

Just as the Bible indicates that copies of the autographs are inspired because they are *graphē* and every *graphē* is inspired, so also can a translation be inspired.

Going back through the fifty appearances of *graphē* in the New Testament, we ask if any of them clearly refer to the Greek Old Testament, which, of course, is a translation. Henry Barclay Swete lists some 160 quotations from the Septuagint in the New Testament.[4] An examination of their contexts reveals that thirteen of these quotations are called *graphē*.

| *New Testament* | *Septuagint* |
| --- | --- |
| Matthew 21:42 (cf. Mark 12:10-11) | Psalm 117:22-23 (118:22-23, Eng.) |
| John 13:18 | Psalm 40:9 (41:9, Eng.) |
| Romans 4:3 | Genesis 15:6 |
| Romans 9:17 | Exodus 9:16 |
| Romans 11:3-4 | 1 Kings 19:10, 14, 18 |
| Galatians 3:8 | Genesis 12:3 |
| Galatians 4:30 | Genesis 21:10 |
| 1 Timothy 5:18 | Deuteronomy 25:4 |
| James 2:8 | Leviticus 19:18 |
| James 4:6 | Proverbs 3:34 |
| 1 Peter 2:6 | Isaiah 28:16 |

Adding Luke 4:18-19, 21 and Acts 8:32-33, the two passages previously mentioned in chapter 3, brings our total to thirteen. There can be no question that the New Testament teaches that the Septuagint is *graphē* and that every *graphē* is inspired.

### Formal Equivalence and Our Theory of Inspiration

Too often and for too long we have ignored conceptual inspiration, zeroing in instead on verbal inspiration. This is true even when we improve our doctrinal statement on inspiration by affirming that it applies to Scripture's *wording*, not merely its *words*. For both the words and the wordings are in Greek and Hebrew and Aramaic and do not survive translation. Therefore, we are bereft of an inspired Bible in any other language, including English.

In order to preserve some modicum of inspiration in the translation, formal equivalence concentrates on the word. To the degree that we have zeroed in on *kai*, for example, to that degree we must endow some favored English word which, acting as *kai*'s surrogate, will in some manner bear the same mantle of inspiration as *kai*. We select *and*. Here we make the mistake of thinking that *kai* is *and* and *and* is *kai*.

Usually, but not always, *and* fits in the English sentence where *kai* fits in the Greek sentence. They are not equivalent, however, but are, rather, circles that overlap a lot. Once an English word is so "frocked" with inspiration, its synonyms, though often better selections, are denied the sacred burden. Listen to the wisdom of the translators of the Authorized Version:

> Another thing we wish to advise you about, gentle reader, is that we have not bound ourselves to any uniformity of phrasing or to any identity of words. Perhaps some, noticing that some scholars have been as exact as possible that way, would wish that we did the same. Most assuredly we were extremely careful. We made it a matter of conscience as was our responsibility. When the word meant the same thing in both places, we did not vary from the sense from what we had translated before. For there are some words that do not have the same meaning everywhere.

> However, it would mince the matter to express the same notion by the same particular word, for example, to translate the Hebrew or Greek word always by "purpose" and never by "intent"; always "journeying" and never "traveling"; "think," but never

"suppose"; "pain," never "ache"; "joy," never "gladness." Such would smack more of fastidiousness than wisdom and would evoke more ridicule from the atheist than profit for the devout reader.

Has the Kingdom of God become words or syllables? Then why should we be in bondage to them when we may be free? Or use one word precisely when another would be no less appropriate?

A godly early church father was quite shaken up when one who likes novelty called a "cot" a "couch." The difference is little or nothing. Another tells how abused he was for changing "gourd," (a reading people had been used to) to "ivy plant." If such happened in better times for so small a reason, we are right to fear severe censure if generally our verbal changes are unnecessary.

On the other hand, we also are charged by scoffers with unequal dealings toward a great number of good English words. For it is said of a certain great philosopher that he should call those logs happy that were made images to be worshipped while their fellow logs, as good as they, went for firewood. We would say as it were to some words, "Stand up higher; have a place in the Bible always," and to others equally as good, "Get you hence; be banished forever." We would be charged possibly with James' words that we are "partial in ourselves and judges of evil thoughts."

Add to this the fact that squeamishness in words has always been counted the next step to trifling. The same is true about fastidiousness in names. Further, we cannot follow a better pattern for style than God Himself. If He used different words in Holy Writ, and indifferently, for the same thing in nature, then we, if we are not superstitious, may take the same liberty in our English translations from Hebrew and Greek.[5]

Our bibliology unconsciously drives us to prefer, if we could have it that way, for every *kai* always to be translated *and*, and would opt for that translation which is most often successful in pulling off the feat. This, I suspect, is the hidden agenda that drives the preference for formal equivalence.

To say "every word in the Bible is inspired" is both ambiguous and inadequate. It is ambiguous because it sounds too much like saying that every word that appears in the Bible is inspired and neglects to qualify the statement with the critical limitation that this is true of that word *only* when it appears in the Bible. For *kai* appears in the Bible. It is therefore inspired. It is also in "The Golden Ass." In fact, about 90 percent of the words appearing in "The Golden Ass" also appear in the Bible. Therefore, 90 percent of "The Golden Ass" is inspired! This idea looks especially ridiculous when we learn that "The Golden Ass" survives as a piece of ancient pornography.

It is inadequate because we really mean "the wording in the Bible is inspired." By this we mean not only the actual words but also their forms and their arrangement. But we do not put a halo around each word. We put a halo around the whole book. Therefore, the statement "Cretans are always liars, evil brutes, lazy gluttons" can be either inspired or not inspired depending on whether we find the statement in Epimenides' *de Oraculis*[6] or in Paul's Epistle to Titus (1:12).

## Inadequate Statements about the Inspiration of the Bible

A significant inadequacy remains to be corrected. If only the wording is inspired, then my Bible, the one I hold in my hands, is not inspired. I mentioned in chapter 2 that language easily divides into two distinct parts: symbol and meaning. I said that the only reason for a symbol to exist is to carry meaning, like boxcars and their cargo. Meaning, therefore, is much more important than symbol. Wording is the symbol and meaning is the load it carries.

*How we came to ignore conceptual inspiration.* Almost a century ago a debate arose over the inspiration of the Bible which separated Christians into two camps: the modernists and the fundamentalists. Modernists asserted that only the thoughts of the Bible were inspired. Fundamentalists, suspecting a hidden agenda (a suspicion which now seems to be vindicated), rallied to the defense of verbal inspiration.

Controversy polarizes, sometimes so much that if we were more rational we would be ashamed of ourselves. Polemics reduce the issue to an either/or proposition: either be a modernist and deny verbal inspiration but espouse conceptual inspiration or be a fundamentalist and espouse verbal inspiration but deny conceptual inspiration.

The controversy, though subsiding considerably, is still here; many still maintain this extreme either/or position. The conservatives (they don't like to be called fundamentalists any more) fail to see that they have made the worse choice. In language, the burden is more important than its vehicle; the meaning it bears is more important than the symbol that bears it.

In the heat of controversy, they failed to see that it is not either/or but both/and. Both the symbol and its meaning are inspired. We cannot say that God has left us with a Bible exactly as he wanted it, concerning whose words and forms and arrangement we dare not tamper, and at the same time say that he couldn't care less about the meanings of those words and forms and arrangement.

When we construct a doctrine of the Bible, our preoccupation with the words to the exclusion of the meanings they bear leads one to suspect that we would have preferred, "In the beginning was the *gramma*, and the *gramma* was with God, and the *gramma* was God." For the emphasis of *logos* is on meaning and of *gramma*, the squiggle on the page.

First, God had something specific in mind which he wanted to communicate to us. Then he chose the proper symbols to do so. We must hold in even higher reverence the meaning he wanted to communicate than the symbols he chose for its vehicle. The vehicle is but a means to an end.

To the degree that I ignore conceptual inspiration, I fight a desperate battle somehow to preserve in the Bible I now hold in my hand some modicum of inspiration in its words. But when I sit down to spell out exactly how my translation is inspired, my typewriter refuses to work. For in all linguistic and semantic honesty, I find myself bereft of any bibliology for my own Bible. Verbal inspiration simply does not survive translation. *But meaning can and does.*

As I discussed in chapter 2, a single word is like a single section of a fence. A combination of words does not necessarily produce meaning any more than many sections of a fence joined together produce a field. As the connected sections must be closed in order to produce a field, so a combination of words must compose a sentence to produce meaning.

The farmer must carefully note the reaches and angles of his closed fence before he can determine the contents of his field. But he does not look at the fence to discover what is growing in the field; he has to examine the field itself.

The translator must take pains to notice every stretch and turn in the wording of the sentence he aspires to translate. Then, however, he must even more carefully continue his examination to determine to the best of his ability the precise meaning that sentence bears.

Then, ignoring the conformation of wording in the source language, he must construct a fence in the receptor language whose reaches and angles might not resemble in the least the reaches and angles of the source language. To the degree that the content of the field the Bible translator has described with his new stretches and turns matches the content of the field described by the reaches and angles in the original Greek or Hebrew, he has produced the inspired word (*logos*, not *gramma*) of God.

## A TRANSLATION WITH POLLUTION
## IS STILL THE WORD OF GOD

It may seem so, but the notion that a translation with pollution is still the word of God is not a new idea. I have already mentioned the preface to the Authorized Version. It addresses this very question: Can a translation containing pollution be the word of God?

> Rather than deny, we actually claim that the poorest translation of the Bible into English offered by Protestants (we see none of the whole Bible offered by Romanists as yet) contains the Word of God, no, *is* the Word of God.

> The king's speech before Parliament, when translated into French, Dutch, Italian and Latin, is still the king's speech although it is not always translated with as good a style or as apt a phrase or exact a sense. For all agree that things take their name from the greater part, and a normal person could say, "When many things in a song are brilliant, I am not offended by a few blemishes." A man may be considered good though he has made many a slip in his life. Otherwise, there are none good, "for in many things we offend all." A good looking man can still have warts on his hands and not only freckles but also scars on his face.

> There is no reason, therefore, why one should deny that a translation is the Word of God or forbid its circulation because some imperfections and blemishes are noticeable in the renderings. What is perfect under the sun? The only exception, of course, are Apostles and apostolic men who were endued with an extraordinary measure of God's Spirit and privileged with infallibility.[7]

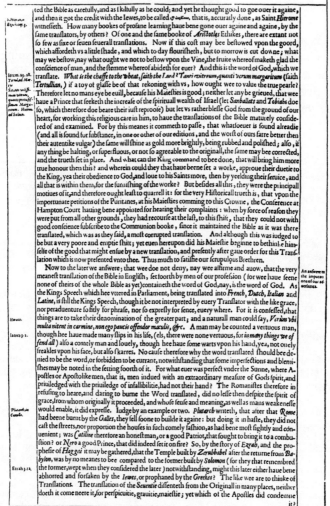

*Sample page from "The Translators to the Reader," the King James Version of The Holy Bible, 1611 edition.*

The amount of pollution intruding the channel coming from translation loss and distortion, though inevitable, can be reduced materially. And the amount coming from inept translators or obsolete translations is being remarkably reduced, for there is an abundance of excellent translations available.

When a Bible student can discover a consensus of meaning (not necessarily of wording) among the best modern translations for a given text, he can be certain that no pollution has occurred in the translation section of the pipe.

---

Chapter 4, Notes

1. Nida has changed his wording from "dynamic equivalence" to "functional equivalence." Jan de Waard and Eugene A. Nida, *From One Language to Another: Functional Equivalence in Bible Translating* (Nashville: Thomas Nelson Publishers, 1986).

2. *Oxford Dictionary of the Christian Church*, 2d ed., s.v. "Purvey, John."

3. The New Testament of this version, known as the Revised Version, was published in England in 1881; the complete Bible followed in 1885. The Revised Version's American counterpart, the American Standard Version, was published in 1901.

4. Henry Barclay Swete, *An Introduction to the Old Testament in Greek*, 2d ed., rev. Richard Rusden Ottley (Cambridge: Cambridge University Press, 1902; reprint ed., New York: Ktav Publishing House Inc., 1968), 382-86.

5. Miles Smith, *The Translators to the Reader: An Introduction to the King James Version of the Bible*, trans. E. W. Goodrick (Portland, Ore.: Multnomah School of the Bible, 1963), 19. Page numbers were not included in the original introduction, but were added in the course of making this translation.

6. Epimenides, *de Oraculis*, or, perhaps, Callimachus's hymn to Zeus. Cf. Kurt Aland et al., eds., *The Greek New Testament*, 3d ed. (n.p.: United Bible Societies, 1975), 740, note to Titus 1:12; A. W. Mair and G. R. Mair, trans., *Callimachus: Hymns and Epigrams; Lycophron; Aratus*, The Loeb Classical Library (Cambridge: Harvard University Press, 1977; London: William Heinemann Ltd., 1977), 36-37; F. J. Foakes Jackson and Kirsopp Lake, eds., *The Beginnings of Christianity Part 1: The Acts of the Apostles*, paperback ed., 5 vols. (Grand Rapids, Mich.: Baker Book House, 1979), vol. 5: *Additional Notes to the Commentary*, ed. Kirsopp Lake and Henry J. Cadbury, 246-51; Martin Dibelius and Hans Conzelmann, *The Pastoral Epistles: A Commentary on the Pastoral Epistles*, ed. Helmut Koester, trans. Philip Buttolph and Adela Yarbro, Hermeneia—A Critical and Historical Commentary on the Bible (Philadelphia: Fortress Press, 1972), 137, n. 15. *De Oraculis* is a Latin translation of the Greek title *peri chrēsmōn*.

Other New Testament quotations from Greek literature are:

"Against such things there is no law" (Galatians 5:23) from Aristotle's *Politics* 3.8.2. Except for a conjunction needed in Aristotle's context but not in Paul's, the Greek is identical.

"For in him we live and move and have our being" (Acts 17:28) from Epimenides' *de Oraculis*. Cf. Lake and Cadbury, 246-51; Richard N. Longenecker, "The Acts of the Apostles," in *The Expositor's Bible Commentary*, ed. Frank E. Gaebelein, 12 vols. (Grand Rapids, Mich.: Zondervan Publishing House, 1976-), 9:476; Ernst Haenchen, *The Acts of the Apostles: A Commentary*, trans. R. McL. Wilson et al. (Philadelphia: The Westminster Press, 1971), 524, n. 3; F. F. Bruce, *The Acts of the Apostles: The Greek Text with Introduction and Commentary*, 2d ed. (Grand Rapids, Mich.: Wm. B. Eerdmans Publishing Co., 1952), 338; Dibelius and Conzelmann, 137, n. 15.

"We are his offspring" (Acts 17:28) from Aratus's *Phaenomena* 5 or, possibly, Cleanthes or Ps-Epimenides. Cf. Kurt Aland et al., eds., *The Greek New Testament*, 3d corrected ed. (n.p.: United Bible Societies, 1983), 487, note to Acts 17:28; Kurt Aland et al., eds., *The Greek New Testament*, (London: United Bible Societies, 1966), 487, note to Acts 17:28; Longenecker, 476; Lake and Cadbury, 246-51; Dibelius and Conzelmann, 137, n. 15.

"Bad company corrupts good character" (1 Corinthians 15:33) from Menander's *Thais*. Cf. Kurt Aland et al., eds., *The Greek New Testament*, 3d ed., 615, note to 1 Corinthians 15:33; W. Harold Mare, "1 Corinthians," in *The Expositor's Bible Commentary*, 10:288.

7. Smith, *Translators to the Reader*, 14.

## RECOMMENDED READING

Knox, Ronald. *The Trials of a Translator*. New York: Sheed & Ward, Inc., 1949.

Nida, Eugene A. *God's Word in Man's Language*. New York: Harper & Bros. Publishers, 1952.

Glassman, Eugene H. *The Translation Debate: What Makes a Bible Translation Good?* Downers Grove, Ill.: Inter-Varsity Press, 1981.

Lewis, Jack P. *The English Bible/from KJV to NIV: A History and Evaluation*. Grand Rapids. Mich.: Baker Book House, 1981.

Waard, Jan de, and Eugene Nida. *From One Language to Another: Functional Equivalence in Bible Translating.* Nashville: Thomas Nelson Publishers, 1986.

Nida, Eugene A., and Charles R. Taber. *The Theory and Practice of Translation.* Helps for Translators Prepared under the Auspices of the United Bible Societies, vol. 8. Leiden: E. J. Brill, 1969.

Beekman, John, and John Callow. *Translating the Word of God: With Scripture and Topical Indexes.* Grand Rapids, Mich.: Zondervan Publishing House, 1974.

## Chapter 5

# *The Interpretations of Your Bible Are Inspired with Drastic Pollution*

*I*t isn't enough to bring the Bible to your hands inspired with very minor pollution. We must go on to take a hard and critical look at how much it gets polluted in the process of transferring it from your hand into your mind, heart, and life.

### THE PROBLEM OF INTERPRETATION POLLUTION

I wish I could say that all the pollution that exists between the pure spring and the faucet lies in the Bible you hold in your hand. Yet I greatly fear that it is into the final section of the pipe—interpretation—that pollution flows unchecked and in quantities far exceeding what is already there, polluting the very water of life we drink. The amount of this pollution is so great that it renders inconsequential the preceding pollution. Still, the situation is not hopeless. The entrance of pollutants at this section of pipe can be sealed off by employing some simple interpretive safeguards.

### The Role of the Exegete

We have talked about the textual critic (chapter 3) and the translator (chapter 4). It is now time to talk about the exegete. You might not know him by this name, but you have met far more of them than you have of both textual critics and translators put together. If you use your Bible, you are one. The Bereans were exegetes also, and Luke records this approvingly, calling them "more noble" (Acts 17:11). An exegete is an interpreter of the Bible. Everyone who uses the Bible is an exegete. Saying this, however, by no means implies the competence of every exegete.

We have mentioned how language divides into two unequal parts: symbol and what is symbolized, wording and meaning, boxcar and its cargo. There is pollution in both places. Because meaning is more important, its pollution is more alarming.

The textual critic strives to reduce pollution, but his sphere of operation lies only in the less important part, the wording. The translator, on the other hand, using the best text the textual critic can produce, strives to translate all of its meaning while introducing as little pollution as he possibly can. Though it is necessary for him to interpret, he must never go out of his way to do so.

The exegete interprets without any such restrictions. In fact, he assays to articulate the whole meaning of the text. He is just as necessary as the textual critic and the translator. For whether it is you yourself or your teacher who does it, unless the Bible is interpreted, it is no more than countless squiggles on reams of pages.

## Our Difficulty in Interpreting the Bible

Whenever you have two or more interpretations to a text, all but one are pollutants, and maybe that one too. Although it shouldn't be all that hard to exegete a passage of Scripture, it seems so sometimes for a number of reasons:

> 1. Perhaps we don't understand the text's external context—the historical, cultural, and geographi-

cal context at the time the prophet spoke or the apostle wrote.

2. Perhaps we ignore the kind of literature that was being spoken or written.

3. Perhaps our doctrine has so preprogrammed us that it has blinded us to the plain meaning of the text.

4. Perhaps the various ways to interpret the text offered by professional exegetes so clutter the landscape that we find it hard to pick the right one out of all the wrong ones.

5. Perhaps we listen to exotic, mystical voices which utter wild and outlandish interpretations, rather than exercise the mind God gave us.

6. Perhaps the shortness of our attention span or our "versitis" leads us to conclusions before the text's context, both literary and historical, has had a chance to inform us. "Versitis" is that disease of compulsion which causes us to jump from one verse to another in violation of the God-given order of progression in his word. There is a remarkable correlation between "verse hopping" and putting the Bible into a theological straitjacket. The biblicist respects the judgment God displayed when he gave us his word in the order found in the Bible. He does not insult God's wisdom by rearranging his order.[1] The cultist, on the other hand, is the champion at "verse hopping."

7. Perhaps our belief in the divine inspiration of the Bible permits us to use rules of interpretation different from the ones used to interpret uninspired literature.

8. Perhaps we use our creativity when exegeting a text.

9. Perhaps the intrusion of neoorthodoxy, which claims that the Bible is the word of God only when it speaks to someone, has led us to the conclusion that the true interpretation of God's word is whatever speaks to us.

10. Perhaps the prestige and the accompanying "ego trip" which come from the discovery of a new interpretation are too great a temptation for the exegete to resist. The status of some Bible teachers is based solely on how much their interpretations differ from the traditional ones.

Actually, the text has but one meaning. Fortunate are we if we find it, however disagreeable and incompatible the true interpretation might appear to be.

## Our Limitations in Interpreting the Bible

Bear in mind that our Lord's patience means salvation, just as our dear brother Paul also wrote you with the wisdom that God gave him. He writes the same way in all his letters, speaking in them of these matters. His letters contain some things that are hard to understand, which ignorant and unstable people distort, as they do the other Scriptures, to their own destruction. (2 Peter 3:15-16)

That the word of God is totally coherent, as coherent as its author, is a conviction based on faith and cannot be empirically arrived at. He who says that the Bible contradicts itself because it appears so to him displays his ignorance either of the enormous competence of its author or, in comparison, of his own abysmal ignorance and displays an overconfidence which borders on arrogance.

We must admit that we fail to solve all the problems of interpretation in the Bible. We should follow the example of the early theologians who threw in the towel when it came to constructing coherent doctrines of the Trinity and the Hypostatic Union. And we should take a lesson from the physicists who have conceded that both the corpuscular and the wavelength theories of light are necessary to account for light's behavior and, yet, in their minds, are not compatible. Their acceptance of both is based on a faith in the coherence of nature and was not empirically arrived at.

We must await the day when we shall "know as well as we are known" before these problems will all be solved—that is, provided that our glorified and sin-unfettered brains will then be competent to trace out all these coherences. In the meantime, we must resolutely stifle our arrogant presumption that we possess enough intelligence to tackle and solve for all time all those apparent contradictions.

## Our Failure to Adhere to the Rules of Interpretation

The wording of the Bible requires interpretation before it can be applied to the life (mind, heart, and deed) of the believer. Here, our sincerity to aggressively defend the purity at the spring is put to the test. How much concern does one also express over pollution in interpretation? When two or more interpretations are offered for a text, all but the true one are mistakes; and all mistakes in interpretation are pollutants. We must reaffirm our commitment to a strict adherence to the rules of interpretation.

All too often, the small group Bible study typifies how not to interpret the Bible. At the home Bible study, someone is asked to read a verse (not a phrase or a clause or a sentence or a paragraph, but a verse, because you wish to remain scriptural). The fact that almost no one has read the verse in preparation can be counted on. The leader then asks, "What does this mean to you?" to which several respond with whatever thoughts come to mind. The answers given often require the leader to exert considerable effort to understand how they could possibly apply and to express delight and encouragement (which unavoidably implies approval) for these expressions of spiritual insight. What a pooling of ignorance and a gross input of pollution!

Maybe what I am about to say is news to you, such a suggestion never having been given you by your pastor, favorite radio Bible teacher, or author—namely, that the text you just read meant something to the very first reader of the autograph or to the very first hearer at the time it was first spoken. This first reader/hearer understood that what he was getting was plain, ordinary communication which employed the ordinary conventions he was used to in day-to-day communication and that he was to arrive at its meaning in the normal manner (albeit probably unconsciously). This is what is supposed to happen to us when we study the Bible.

The first reader/hearer surely didn't consider the verse a catalyst to trigger a different revelatory reaction in each mind, with each reaction equally as relevant and true! And, unless the writer/speaker is playing word games, only one interpretation is true. Waard and Nida say "the primary exegetical perspective of a translator is 'what did the text mean to people who were the original receptors?' "[2]

Furthermore, with no control over what a text means—for many say that meaning is not inspired, remember?—we become vulnerable to a hermeneutical anarchy that makes the Bible mean about anything a person wishes as long as that person reveres the text. Thus we open a floodgate for catastrophic amounts of pollution to enter the stream.

Divine inspiration viewed with the larger implication that it covers meaning as well as wording brings down such an awful and solemn charge upon how we interpret the text that it will never again be possible to be precise about our definition of verbal, plenary, inerrant Scriptures and be careless about our hermeneutics. "Not many of you should presume to be teachers, my brothers, because you know that we who teach will be judged more strictly," says James (3:1).

## BASIC RULES FOR INTERPRETATION

*Hermeneutics* is a technical term for those principles which direct a person to the right meaning of a text. The first reader/hearer probably would not be able to spell out the rules for interpreting ordinary communication. But if we should do so for him, he would say, "Of course." And these rules would be so simple they would go without saying.

And though you, a modern-day reader of that same text, may not be able to articulate the rules for interpreting communication, if I would do it for you, they would be so simple they would go without saying. And they would be the same rules the first reader/hearer used. If you went by them, you would arrive at the same meaning the first reader/hearer did, and you would be right!

## The Questionable Quest for
## Authorial Intent

To inquire into what the author meant when he said something seemed to me at the start to be eminently sensible. However, three compelling facts have required me to give up the quest for authorial intent.

First, when a composition is the work of two authors—in the Bible, they are the human and the divine authors—am I asking the human or am I asking the divine author what his intent was?

Second, I am quite certain that at some times, perhaps even occasionally, the human author did not understand what he was saying (1 Peter 1:10-12; Job 42:3; Daniel 8:27; 12:8; cf. Numbers 12:6, 8).

> Concerning this salvation, the prophets, who spoke of the grace that was to come to you, searched intently and with the greatest care, trying to find out the time and circumstances to which the Spirit of Christ in them was pointing when he predicted

the sufferings of Christ and the glories that would follow. It was revealed to them that they were not serving themselves but you, when they spoke of the things that have now been told you by those who have preached the gospel to you by the Holy Spirit sent from heaven. Even angels long to look into these things.

(1 Peter 1:10-12)

And when this is the case, how can we ask him what his intent was?

And third, I am developing an abhorrence to any move on the part of finite man to inquire into God's motives for doing what he does. Unless he tells us what we do not know, there is no way we can be confident of the truth of our surmises. And even when he gives us a reason, we do not know all his intent.

So I feel a lot safer avoiding inquiry into authorial intent. Because it is a given that God is the perfect communicator, I think we can accomplish our objective by inquiring *what was the first reader/hearer's understanding of the meaning of what God said*. By this, I don't totally exclude authorial intent, for it will surface when, crawling inside the skin of the first reader/hearer, we must endeavor to sense what were his feelings about the character, personality, and beliefs of the writer/speaker.

## Common Sense Principles of Interpretation

The following, then, are nine common sense principles for getting the unpolluted meaning from your Bible:

*1. Use your common sense.*

The inspired writer wrote in an ordinary language where common sense prevailed. This principle governs all other principles of interpretation. So, if any one of the eight remaining principles fails to commend itself to your common sense, you would be well advised to reject it.

As already mentioned, God is a master communicator. Good communicators use the language and vocabulary of the people they talk to, and if they are honest, they also attach the same meanings to the words that their hearers do. Since God is honest, it is common sense that he has done the same.

So it is common sense to interpret the Bible the same way you would any other book. How else could the first reader do it? This is true even though the Bible is incalculably more important than the best books mankind has produced.

The exegete would be greatly helped if he would read Mortimer J. Adler and Charles Van Doren's *How to Read a Book* (revised and updated edition, 1972) and, for the intellectually adventurous person, E. D. Hirsch Jr.'s *Validity in Interpretation* (1967). These books explain how to get the meaning from any book.

### 2. *Be simple.*

Daniel Webster, in his *Confession of Faith*, said the following:

> I believe that the Bible is to be understood and received in the plain and obvious meaning of its passages; since I cannot persuade myself that a book intended for the instruction and conversion of the whole world, should cover its true meaning is [sic] such mystery and doubt, that none but critics and philosophers can discover it.[3]

Your first goal is to discover how the first reader understood the text. His method was so simple he didn't need an exegete. In fact, the first reader at Philippi needed an exegete to explain to him what Paul meant about as badly as a cowboy needed a lawyer to explain to him what the cook meant when he hollered, "Come-an-git-it!"

Once we have managed to crawl inside the first reader's skin and are able to read the Bible with his eyes, it is all quite simple and easy. Getting into that skin is an entirely different matter. It is so extremely difficult that nobody is completely successful. To learn to look at the first reader's world through his eyes, understand his language, live his experience of the reception and reading of that epistle, to love and respect the sender as much as he, to have the memories of contact and fellowship with him, is not simple. But this is not interpretation; it is a necessary prelude to it. After one gets inside that skin, interpretation is simple.[4]

*3. Go with the flow.*

The right meaning of a text is the one that fits most comfortably into the writer's flow of thought up to, into, in, out of, and beyond the text. This includes not only the immediately preceding and following sentences but also extends all the way to the beginning and to the end of the book, diminishing in import as the distance from the target text grows.

The context can embellish the target text by elaborating on it, illustrating it, or supplying the paragraph of which it is the topic sentence. On the other hand, it may distract from it, limit its application, alter it, or even reverse its meaning.

Always make the target text and the immediate contexts, both before and after, complete sentences. This means you must ignore chapters and verses. They were not part of the original, but were added much later—chapters by Stephen Langton at the beginning of the thirteenth century, Old Testament verses by Rabbi Isaac Nathan in about 1440, and New Testament verses by Robert Stephanus in 1551.[5] Of course, the Book of Psalms is not divided into chapters but is composed of discrete psalms.

This rule about the context is the rule most violated by cultists and fledgling Bible students. "A text, taken out of its context, becomes a pretext" is an often repeated statement because it is so true.

*4. Stay within language conventions.*

Go with the usual way wording works and with what words mean.

*How wording works.* Unless you know Hebrew and Greek well enough to scan them, you are still dependent upon their translation. And even if a person knows those languages that well, it wouldn't hurt for him to read how translators have construed the text.

A telltale mark betraying his ineptitude is the untrained Bible student's emphasis upon words to the neglect of wording. That is, he exhibits a proneness to investigate the meaning of individual words at the expense of investigating how those words work together to create meaning. He manifests an inability to handle the language's syntax.

Be thankful if you were trained in high school to diagram sentences. Now practice this art in your Bible study. There is a hierarchy among sentence slots. The verb, subject, direct object, and indirect object, in that order, are more important than the adverb, adjective, preposition, and conjunction, in that order. This determines the degree of attention we give each sentence slot. Subordinate clauses are generally not as important as main clauses.

Notice where the paragraphs begin and end. Four of the five Bibles I recommend for choices for one's main Bible indent only at paragraphs. And the one that doesn't has used a paragraph marker by bold-facing the verse number where a paragraph begins.

*What words mean.* Again, if you do not know Greek and Hebrew, use a good English dictionary, Bible dictionary, and concordance. Look up the word in these reference tools. Words usually have more than one meaning. In any appearance of a certain word in the Bible, attribute only one of the dictionary's meanings to it. And do not attribute the definition that *you* prefer or that is more doctrinally amenable (to your doctrine, of course), but the meaning that fits into the flow. Only when the author is deliberately making a play on words—very rare in the Bible—is more than one meaning per word intended.

The vast majority of words in any language are pastel words. Psychedelic words are always rare. For instance, the Greek pastel words *dynamis* and *logos* appear about 120 and 330 times respectively in the New Testament. Most of the time, *dynamis* should be translated by the pastel English word *ability*, and its verb form, *dynamai*, by the pastel English word *can*. And often, *logos* should be translated by the pastel English word *thing*.

On the other hand, the Greek psychedelic words *thriambeuō* and *metamorphoō* appear two and four times respectively in the New Testament. *Metamorphoō* means to "transform," and *thriambeuō* means to be given a "ticker tape" parade.

There is a noticeable tendency on the part of those whose Bible exposition is composed mainly of words to make pastel words psychedelic. This is polluting, not expounding, the text. Gilding the lily is an occupational disease of the inept exegete.

Translators do not make it a rule to translate a Greek or Hebrew word always with the same English word. So an English concordance cannot be relied upon to present an accurate spread of a word in Greek or Hebrew. When studying a single word, use a dictionary to discover not only that word's definitions but also its synonyms and antonyms and their definitions. Then look those words up in your concordance as well.

*5. See the text as a revelatory event.*

Understand that a writing and its reading, the preaching and its hearing, happened in a particular kind of culture at a certain time and place by a certain writer or speaker, usually to a particular people or person for a particular purpose. Your attention should not be limited to the text, but should embrace the whole revelatory event when that text was first read or heard. You have to crawl inside the skin of a person in that first audience. This is the historical context, the *Sitz im Leben*.

Don't give up on this effort simply because it is so difficult. Remember, any progress lessens the amount of pollution you contribute to the very word of God. So keep on studying history, geography, archaeology, and the culture and language of the peoples of the Bible.

I am not contradicting what I said in rule #2. What I said there was that to the first reader/hearer, getting what was meant was easy. The same is true for us once we get inside the reader's/hearer's skin. Getting in there is the difficulty, but

getting in there is not hermeneutics. It is, rather, the e
one needs before one can "do" hermeneutics.

The covenant prevailing at the time the text is compos
is an important element in the text's historical context. A covenant is a contract when God is a contracting party. The first
reader/hearer would understand what he is learning in the light
of his relationship with God as expressed in the covenant he
is under. This would be very important to him.

A text, taken out of its historical context, is also a pretext.

## 6. *See the text as a part of the whole.*

The technical name for this principle is the *analogy of
faith*. Common sense tells us that when we are trying to understand someone, we should assume that he is not contradicting
himself and that the better we know someone the better we
understand what he means. We should reluctantly arrive at the
conclusion that the author has contradicted himself only after
we have tried hard and have failed to find an interpretation
compatible with the context that would be consistent with the
author's known beliefs. The burden of proof lies with the person
who claims that a contradiction exists.

*Danger! Proceed with utmost caution!* Among professional exegetes, this is the most abused of all the principles
of interpretation I am listing. Though we limit this tenet to the
work of the author, we find it impossible, for theological
reasons, to live under such restrictions. For if God ultimately
is responsible for the whole Bible, he, in a very real sense, is
its author, and our assumption has to be that when we interpret
the Bible correctly, no part of it contradicts any other part.

I can live with this reasoning, provided I stop here and
do not add that we should be able to harmonize the Bible
completely. For we should not presume we have either the
knowledge or the intellectual powers to solve all the problem
passages in the Bible. We have already learned to live with
gray areas and unsolved problems. We have already given up
on the Trinity, the Hypostatic Union, and (at least biblicists
have and dearly wish everybody else would) the tension between man's free will and God's sovereignty.

ng line to be drawn across the slippery
en the principle that an author is to be
adicting himself and the principle that
considered true is the one that is doctri-

ful, one finds oneself sliding from the
top to the bottom. We derive our doctrine from the Bible, and
our doctrine represents the best attempt we are able to make
at summarizing and organizing the meanings of the Bible. So
the second way of expressing this rule seems, without careful
thought, to be better than the first. But when this rule of the
analogy of faith becomes the tail that wags the dog, we know
we have become victims of this slippery slope.

Mainly, our doctrine did not come inductively and subliminally from our own constant rereading of the Bible. We got
it from a doctrine book which was laced with biblical proof
texts. And because the proof texts seemed to agree, we jumped
to the conclusion that it represented truthfully the meaning of
the Bible.

Mainly, Christian doctrine arises out of intramural controversy between Christian sects. Both sides—they rarely convince one another—formulate their divergent beliefs about that
controversy and fortify them with biblical proof texts. So one
doctrine book rarely serves well more than one sect.

When statements are made on the same subject in different
places in the Bible, obviously they must be studied together.
When the subject in the target text is oblique or obscure but
is made direct or clear in another location, common sense tells
us to accede to the meaning of the other text.

A lot of pollution enters here when an exegete is confronted with a statement whose meaning opposes his doctrine.
He tends to view the text's meaning as obscure and, therefore,
accedes with a clear conscience to a contrary text with whose
meaning he is in doctrinal agreement. Another exegete, with
a contrary doctrine, would, with an equally clear conscience,
simply reverse the roles of those very texts.

Just because the meaning of a text is contrary to one's
doctrine does not mean that it is obscure. The statement "He

is the atoning sacrifice for our sins, and not only for ours but also for the sins of the whole world" (1 John 2:2) most definitely is not an obscure text, even though it denies outright a doctrine held dearly by many sincere Christians.[6]

So dangerous is this principle that I counsel fledgling exegetes not to use it. It is our chief source of pollution.

*7. Keep in mind the genre of the text you are interpreting.*

No matter where you turn in your Bible, you will be reading a particular kind of literature. Each kind of literature is called a *genre*. The kind of literature your target text is cannot help but affect the meaning of the text. If it is a parable, the event was not historical. If it is poetry, one must emphasize what two parallel lines have in common, not their distinctions. The historical context contributes far less to the Book of Proverbs than it does to Philemon because proverbs have a general and universal application. So it is important for the serious Bible student to determine the genre of the text he is studying and to keep in mind the ways in which that genre affects meaning.

There are two general kinds of genres: one which characterizes a composition and one which is embedded in a composition. For example, the designations "letter" and "gospel" describe compositions, whereas metaphors and parables are found in compositions. A poem can be a composition, as in the Psalms and Lamentations, or a part of a composition, as in Jeremiah and Ezekiel.

Genre compositions found in the Bible include the following:

| | |
|---|---|
| Narrative | like Genesis |
| Prophecy/Preaching | like Isaiah |
| Didactic/Legal | like Leviticus |
| Epistle | like Colossians |
| Apocalyptic | like Revelation |
| Poetry | like Psalms |
| Wisdom | like Proverbs |

(The gospels are a subdivision under narrative.)

Strangely, hermeneutics has neglected the study of the contributions genre makes toward meaning. But this is now changing. An excellent and popularly written book which goes into this subject is Gordon D. Fee and Douglas Stuart's *How to Read the Bible for All Its Worth: A Guide to Understanding the Bible* (1982).

*8. Be sympathetic to the text.*

What one says must be understood in the framework of what one believes. So if you are really trying to understand what someone means, you must look at it as coming from his world view.

Interpretation is not evaluation. The interpreter does not say how good or true something is, only what that person meant when he said or wrote it. In order to do this, he must understand how what that person said or wrote is the result of the interaction between the data he presents and his presuppositions.

You can't interpret *Hamlet* unless, temporarily at least, you believe in ghosts. Sympathy with a text—as opposed to feelings of hostility—is prerequisite to a true interpretation of a text by Paul the apostle or by Karl Marx.

*9. Pray that the Holy Spirit will guide your thinking.*

Is it not one of the ministries of the Holy Spirit to enlighten us about what the Bible means? And if so, wouldn't his interpretation be without pollution? To both questions, I must answer, "Yes."

But the Holy Spirit does not operate as many suppose. He does not inform us by any mystical nudge, impulse, "gut feeling," or "voice." More often than not—I resist the temptation to say always—these subjective emotions and thoughts are sacrilegiously attributed to the Holy Spirit.

Rather, he, in response to our prayer for guidance, moves upon us so skillfully that we are not even conscious of what he is doing and so manipulates our thought processes that his interpretations make sense to us.

The teacher who takes seriously James's "we who teach will be judged more strictly" (3:1) is motivated by fear to repeat constantly the prayer in Psalm 119:18, "Open my eyes that I may see wonderful things in your law."

The interpreter must first believe—without any confirmation—that God has answered his prayer and then must proceed to exercise his mental powers to their maximum in order to exploit to the full that which issues from those Spirit-directed powers. He must exploit this with confidence and without fear. The Holy Spirit is no substitute for industry. He fructifies industry.

## SOURCES OF POLLUTION

If it's all that easy, then why all this pollution? Let me offer some reasons why interpretation pollutes to an intolerable degree.

### Elitist Exegesis

There is the unfounded belief that because the Bible is God's communication, the means by which he chose to communicate must be different from the ordinary ways in which we communicate. Therefore, there must be some esoteric key which unlocks the Bible's deeper meaning.

This gives rise to an elitist class that has discovered this key and to which all the rest of us are beholden for the "deeper meaning of the word." Unfortunately, this class does not attract the best of us to join. It perpetuates itself by continually feeding this myth and pollutes God's word in disgraceful proportions.

I have been studying the Bible for more than fifty years and have been making my living at it for more than forty. If I have learned anything, I know there are no deeper meanings in the Bible, only surface meanings, the implications of which are often so profound that the best of us cannot sound them all, yet whose basic sense is so simple the wayfaring man, even the fool, need not err therein.

## Cultural Pollution

Human nature is the same, whether the person is a Papua New Guinean, an Eskimo, a New York apartment dweller, or the first reader/hearer. We all have to breathe, eat, find shelter, copulate, educate. We all hurt; feel pleasure; love; hate; fear; joke; adore children; abhor incest; value family; respect knowledge; revere wisdom; wonder; reach out to the Supernatural; play; sing; dance; decorate; laugh; cry; quarrel; cooperate; are gregarious, yet either submissive or dominant; are conscious of the difference between mine and yours, ours and theirs; are status conscious. People are amazingly alike.

The list goes on and on. But what I have enumerated contains all that is important to the human condition. The heart of biblical teaching ministers to these characteristics. We don't have to adapt the most important teachings of the Bible to other cultures. They are universally appropriate.

We are only different in culture (and language is an essential part of culture). This fact is especially important because, in this existential age, people think they are so essentially different that they must reinterpret the Bible to make it relevant for today.

However, to ignore culture is to open the gates for large quantities of pollution to enter. For the Bible is married to the Semitic culture of the Middle East. Especially, ethical teachings must be justified by the character of that culture and may be applied to a different culture only where it resembles the biblical one.

It is impossible in our sedentary and law-abiding culture to practice the biblical laws of hospitality. They were made for nomadic and lawless cultures. Yet, we still make efforts to do so by changing, without getting permission, the meaning of the word. The word does not mean entertaining for Sunday dinner the newcomer in church. Biblical hospitality is the compulsion on the part of the host to house, feed, and protect the traveler.

At times, understanding the biblical culture may be difficult. But it is important enough to make the effort. The first reader/hearer had a nature like yours and mine. The reason you and I identify so with Odysseus and Joseph is that they are you and me with different clothes on.

## Theological Pollution

Another breach by which pollution enters, against which all Christians must be warned, is theology.

No one should or can avoid doctrine, especially among us westerners who have been so trained as not to be able to think in any other way than as Aristotle thought. For us, I say, and perhaps for everybody, doctrine is necessary. As we mature in our Bible knowledge we will want to, and should, study doctrine per se.

The Bible comes first, then doctrine. The Bible is the dog; doctrine the tail. When the tail wags the dog, you have serious pollution, if I may mix my metaphors.

We cannot at the same time take our doctrine from the Bible and take our doctrine to the Bible. When we do the latter, the Bible becomes a servant to our doctrine. And then the Bible student studies his Bible until he can make it come out right, that is to say, until the meaning of its wording supports his doctrine. His Bible is slowly transformed into a repository of proof texts which support his theology.

This might seem quite innocent, until we notice that the people in the church across the street—who match our zeal and our claim that the Bible is infallible and our sole guide to belief and practice—have polluted the landscape with false doctrine based upon an invalid interpretation of the biblical texts.

And the people in the church a half a mile down the road, claiming to get their doctrine from the same source, introduce a different set of pollutants from other invalid deductions from the text. In fact, ours is the only church in town that doesn't pollute the Scripture. I get this straight from my pastor, who has shown conclusively from the Bible that we are right and they are wrong. But why are so many of them wrong and so few of us right?

I exclude from the above those sects in Christendom which have a special prophet who interprets the Scriptures so authoritatively that his or her writing becomes part of Scripture. I am thinking of prophets like Joseph Smith, Mary Baker Eddy, Ellen G. White, Pastor Russell, and Reverend Moon. I am not talking about *that* pollution. I am talking about the pollution in churches well within the parameters of orthodoxy.[7]

Perhaps doctrine sometimes gets too big for its britches. Controversy makes mountains out of mole hills. So one involved in intense controversy begins to believe that the doctrine he espouses is about as important as any other, something he would have been embarrassed to have believed before the controversy began.

For example, let me take two doctrines espoused within my own communion. The first is this: Jesus Christ is God as much as our Heavenly Father and he participated with him in the creation of the universe. The second says this: All genuinely born-again Christians will either be resurrected or raptured from the earth before the Great Tribulation.

These two doctrines differ between themselves in two significant ways. The first difference is the emphasis the Bible itself places on them. It is the more humble position to adopt the priorities of the Bible for our own, and a rough and ready way to list the biblical ones is to go by the relative amount of time the Bible devotes to each of its doctrines. This is not to say that one is more true than the other, but that one is more important than the other. Without a doubt, the deity of Christ is far more important than the sequencing of the First Resurrection and the "time of Jacob's trouble."

The second difference is how much these two doctrines differ with respect to their general acceptance among all Bible believers. The first is universal, being held by all believers who go by the Bible alone. But the second is held by a minority—some would say a small minority—of Bible believers.

One added caution. Although Jesus is God, it does not follow that every interpretation of a text that teaches his deity is, therefore, a true interpretation. He clearly identified himself

with Yahweh. However, this does not allow us to read identifi-
cation with Yahweh into every text where he uses the words
"I am"—as in "I am the good shepherd" (John 10:14). Although
it may not pollute the doctrine, it certainly pollutes the text.
On the other hand, there is no question that the insistence upon
a particular sequence between the eschatological resurrection
and tribulation introduces pollution. Of course, each side thinks
the other is causing the pollution.

May I, with extreme apprehension, suggest that just
maybe we have become overextended in our dogmatic doctrinal
statements and that if we could find some way to save face,
we might retreat to those doctrines held more universally
throughout the history of the church. This would reduce the
peer pressure on us to use force, if necessary, to bring the Bible
into conformity with the true doctrine, namely, that of our own
communion (of course).

## The Proliferation of Interpretive Options

By "interpretive options" I mean the multiplication of
choices of what a given text might mean. If you are a layman
relying upon a professional clergyman's word for it when it
comes to the meaning of a text, let me let you in on the
existence of a not too well known fact.

This custodianship over what Christianity is and what the
Bible is and what the Bible means is three-tiered. You don't
have to be told that you are on the bottom. But you also need
to know that your professional clergyman is only on the second
tier. For he himself is subject to his academic betters who
taught him and who teach from such academic heights that the
poor student rarely aspires to climb them.

In this rather rarefied atmosphere, an academic fraternity
exists whose loyalties to each other altogether too often outrank
any loyalty to "the faith that was once for all entrusted to the
saints."[8] Courtesy toward fellow members and their children
is not only expected of these gentlemen, but also any lack
thereof is a just reason for expulsion. By *children*, I mean the
new interpretations their academic endeavors produce. You just

don't go around denigrating other people's children. What they have begotten must be treated with courtesy and even praised and any of its malformations criticized with extreme caution.

At first glance, this might be considered an expression of Christian grace. Actually, it is tit for tat. You be kind to my children and I will be kind to yours. By this reciprocal praise, we not only will raise each other in our own fraternity but will also raise the status of our own fraternity among the fraternities of academia.

In the biblical community, this self-serving custom translates into a multiplying of interpretations. Since in other fraternities advancement is determined by creativity, the temptation is great in the biblical community to engage one's creativity in the interpretation of a text. Actually, there is no room for creativity when interpreting what someone else says. But these interpretive options are dignified into viable interpretations through the respect given them by the other scholars who, out of self-preservation, have entered into a pact of mutual admiration.

Every such interpretation proliferates pollution. Passed down through the tiers, they present themselves like a cafeteria line which one may go down selecting the interpretation that meets one's personal preference, like stewed prunes instead of coleslaw. And we know that stewed prunes and coleslaw are both true.

Fortunately, stupid interpretations do have a limited life span and eventually die. Unfortunately, however, those dwelling in the highest tier have a rather lazy way to reduce the number of aspirants to their fraternity. The aspirant must write a dissertation in which he must demonstrate his competence to do research. In this research, he is obliged to disinter all of the deceased theories, do an autopsy on them, and then re-inter them, further perpetuating pollutants. To miss any one theory is to put one's initiation at risk.

Graders find this inventorying of interpretive options much easier to grade than any discernment the aspirant displayed when he selected the theories he judged worthy of review and ignored those he deemed not worthy of notice. Many a polluting interpretation that deserves a death with dignity is kept alive by the heroic efforts of that life-support apparatus called a footnote.

In spite of all this, there do remain texts so difficult to interpret that no interpretation yet offered commends itself to a general consensus. Here, the exegete must legitimately seek for new interpretive options, even though he is aware that he may be proliferating pollutants, because he lives in the hope that the only true interpretation may yet be discovered.

## WHAT CAN WE DO ABOUT POLLUTION?

Transmission pollution can be diminished by gifted men and women devoting themselves to the continuing discipline of textual criticism. Translation pollution can be diminished by everyone adopting that translation which has the least pollutants. Interpretation pollution can be diminished by the creation and maintenance of a new prestigious fraternity of biblicists whose commitment to the inspiration of the *meanings* of the Bible and to the rules for their discovery is compulsive. Interpretation pollution can be further diminished by the dedication of the general body of Christ to these same two commitments and to the development of its own spiritual perception of good interpretations so that it will no longer fall victim to incompetent teachers.

Communions existing because of a differing Christian theology are a stench in the nostrils of God. The rejection of the biblical cry for unity is one of our most serious pollutants. A little more tolerance for the church across the street and the way it interprets a text is needed. And a little more humility on our part when we do a self-evaluation of our own exegetical skills wouldn't do any harm. Does it have to be that when they interpret a verse differently, they are always wrong and we are always right?

Some way must be found to break the stranglehold theology has on our interpretation of a text. Isn't there a role for biblicists who would deny theology this privilege? I do not suggest that the biblicist should have no theology—that would be both harmful and impossible—but that he insist that the Bible rule over his theology.

Moreover, we must turn our love for biblical interpretive options into hate and cry out that only one of them, if any at all, is true and the rest are pollutants. Inventorying them all is not erudition.

Also, if the pew-run Christian would acquaint himself with the ABCs of the rules of interpretation and would practice them in his Bible study, he would develop a discernment adequate enough to challenge sleazy exegesis and would demand quality work on the part of his teachers.

It is extremely important to understand the role of the gifted teacher and to be able to discern between the good teacher and the poor teacher. The task of the gifted teacher is twofold. First, he must help the present believer over the impediments caused by the distance in culture which separates him from the first reader/hearer. Second, he must try to integrate his target text into the whole of God's counsel. Because the teacher is given this charisma from God, he is so highly privileged as to deserve "double honor" (1 Timothy 5:17), a privilege, I might add, not without considerable risk (James 3:1). The rest of God's people are well advised to take advantage of this gifted person.[9]

I only wish it wasn't necessary to warn you to proceed with caution and to be like the Bereans, who examined the Scriptures daily themselves to see whether or not what they were being taught was so (Acts 17:11).

Search for a teacher who is humble and honest, or better, honest and humble. Look for one who has a great imagination but who *never*, I say *never*, exercises his creativity while in the process of reading "from the Book of the Law of God" and "making it clear and giving the meaning" (Nehemiah 8:8).

For his creativity always competes with the author's creativity, whose creativity alone he should be seeking to describe. The only decent attitude for the gifted teacher is to stand barefoot and afraid because he is standing on holy ground (cf. Exodus 3:5-6).

## Chapter 5, Notes

1. The Bible is not a book wherein you start at page one and read consecutively through to the end. It is, rather, a library of books, the order of which, to a large extent, is arbitrary. So my insistence on maintaining the biblical order lies solely within the individual books. We would be more faithful to God's original order if we would restore Samuel, Kings, and Chronicles to a single title each and Ezra/Nehemiah and Luke/Acts to two-volume works. The Jewish order of the Old Testament books is different from the Christian order. And when the earliest manuscripts of the New Testament are examined, one discovers that the order of its books also varies.

2. Jan de Waard and Eugene A. Nida, *From One Language to Another: Functional Equivalence in Bible Translating* (Nashville: Thomas Nelson Publishers, 1986), 177.

3. Frank S. Mead, ed. and comp., *Encyclopedia of Religious Quotations* (London: Peter Davies Ltd., 1965), 34.

4. However, we are not through with the "first reader/hearer" once we have crawled inside the Christian of Philippi and have read the epistle through his eyes. For it is eminently reasonable to suppose that one who has had access to the whole counsel of God, the completed canon of Scripture, would understand any part of it better than the person who knew only the text that was written to him.

So we must construct a second cadre of "first readers/hearers," those who would be able to approach any text with the information derived from all the Scripture. Certainly a person who has the advantage of the New Testament would understand further implications of Isaiah 7:14 which would not have entered the minds of King Ahaz and his courtiers.

So one must crawl inside the skins of two "first readers/hearers": first and most important, the reader/hearer who possesses only the text addressed to him and, after that, the "first reader/hearer" who approaches the text from the vantage point of acquaintance with the whole canon. And this second reader/hearer must never be allowed to contradict the first, but only to embellish him.

I stoutly resist the notion of a third cadre of "first readers/hearers," those who in their lifetime would have had the time to allow the congealed theology welling up subliminally to inform a given text, though I must admit the idea has some strong attractions. For it would seem necessary to allow all the new data of the New Testament time to ferment so that its new perceptions could congeal. I worry about the length of time required though. To me, the early church took altogether too much time to congeal the Trinity and the

Hypostatic Union. I don't think we should allow the decisions of Chalcedon and Nicaea to inform us about the composition of the "faith" in Jude 3, although they may, even should, inform our theology.

5. Bruce M. Metzger, *Manuscripts of the Greek Bible: An Introduction to Greek Palaeography* (New York: Oxford University Press, 1981), 41-42.

6. I'm referring, of course, to the "limited atonement" doctrine of Calvinism. Likewise the text "you are Peter, and on this rock I will build my church" (Matthew 16:18) is not in the least bit obscure. One only needs to ask a Hindu or a Buddhist or a Muslim or an atheist to read it, and he would tell you. And they would all agree, especially if they took the time to get into the flow of thought before and after the text. And yet, torturous exercises are endured in order to produce some other interpretation of this statement simply because what it obviously means is out of sync with our theology!

7. If those called to teach would study and apply the information found in Moises Silva's book, *Biblical Words and Their Meaning: An Introduction to Lexical Semantics* (Grand Rapids, Mich.: Zondervan Publishing House, 1983), a considerable portion of this kind of pollution would be avoided.

8. Jude 3. Grammarians and commentators agree that "the faith," *hē pistis,* here, as in some other places (Galatians 1:23; 3:23-25; 1 Timothy 4:1, 6; 6:21; etc.), is the *fides quae creditur,* "the doctrine." To suggest that Jude meant the doctrine after Luther or even after Augustine or Chalcedon or Nicaea would be a gross anachronism. What Jude had in mind and what his readers understood "the faith" to be would have been substantially less than that. After a serious attempt to identify "the faith" by a historical investigation of it in Jude's day, one concludes that what is worth fighting over are the bare bones of essential Christianity—an entity few if any of today's theologians are, by virtue of their training or research, competent to identify.

9. Perhaps what appears to be a contradiction between John and Paul is not a contradiction after all. John says that the pew-run Christian doesn't need anyone to teach him (1 John 2:27) whereas Paul establishes the office of teacher to edify pew-run Christians (Ephesians 4:11-12; 1 Corinthians 12:28-29; Romans 12:5-7; et al.).

John is justified because the quality of the communication to the first reader/hearer made it easy for him to understand the text. However, the Holy Spirit anticipated the universality and longevity of the church wherein the pew-run Christian, growing more and more remote, could not be expected to crawl into the first reader's/hearer's skin. So he supplies him with the gifted teacher who by his education can supplement the reader's surface understanding by teaching him the text's historical context and the translation's loss and distortion. If, as I have asserted, because of the universality of human nature, today's pew-run Christian is the same as the first reader/hearer, only with different clothes on, then the teacher, building on what the present reader has already learned, embellishes and sharpens it, supplies nuances for it, and enlarges its implications.

Harmonizing John and Paul in this way creates a danger. It is too easy to overlook the fact that the present reader has already discovered the essence of the text's meaning and that what the teacher adds are only supplements to it. The glamorous contributions of the gifted teacher might overshadow this essence. The teacher must never overlook where the downbeat comes.

# Conclusions

*You can have confidence in the Bible you hold in your hand.*

I hope you see by now that the pollution of the Bible in your hand is minuscule compared to the pollution it receives after coming to your hand. To exercise concern over the present state of the text without at the same time hitting the ceiling at the way its message is too often mishandled is an inconsistency not short of hypocrisy.

It would be folly for a chronic smoker to be more concerned over the pollution of the earth's atmosphere than he is over the pollution of the air in his own lungs. It is precisely the same with you, dear traveler with me through these pages. Your concern over the inspiration of the Scripture, its inerrancy and infallibility, must never exceed your concern over the amount of pollution that contaminates the word of God when it is ingested by you or by those you teach.

And if you are among that privileged few who do preach and teach this sacred truth, I must ask, How much of a source of pollution are you to those you teach because they trustfully ingest what you are saying? Since those who teach will be

**111**

judged more strictly (James 3:1), take all the effort it requires to insure that what you teach comes solely from that store of meanings that the best translations supply. Learn to hate pollution with a holy hatred.

What version do you hold in your hand? My own nominees—I think the consensus of people in the know who have no ax to grind would agree—for the five best modern English translations are the Jerusalem Bible, Today's English Version, the Revised Standard Version, the New American Standard Bible, and the New International Version (these are not given in any order).[1] I hope the Bible you hold in your hand is one of these five.

When studying a particular text, getting a consensus of its meaning (not its wording) from a comparison of all five of the above translations will give you more pollutant-free meaning than ten years of Greek study. I say this even though I love my Greek Testament dearly and have made my living for thirty years teaching it. If I have an ax to grind, I am acting contrary to it.

## Please Don't Maltreat This Book

If the only benefit you have received from this book is the impetus to increase the volume of your condemnation of the practice of those of other theological persuasions, you have prostituted and profaned what I have tried to do. I have probably done you more harm than good. What I really wanted to do was to bring you under such conviction that:

1. You will develop a strong aversion to interpretive options;
2. You will pray for integrity as you examine what the Bible says;
3. Your submission to the lordship of Christ will extend to what he says;
4. Your hierarchy of values will require that you be comfortable with your Bible and uncomfortable

with your theology rather than comfortable with
your theology and uncomfortable with your
Bible.

## Your Bible Is the Inspired
## Word of God

You can trust your Bible, for it is the inspired word of
God. The pollution which intruded in the transmission and
translation of the Bible is minor, under control, and diminishing. Therefore, your Bible is trustworthy.

My concern for you is that after hearing that copies and
translations of the Bible cannot be inerrant and infallible, you
will conclude that they cannot be the inspired word of God
because you have been told that inspiration implies both infallibility and inerrancy. If inerrancy and infallibility are necessary
qualities of inspiration, then only the autographs are inspired.
I should have said *were* inspired, for as far as we know (and
we can be pretty sure of it) none of these autographs exists.
If inspiration is limited to the autographs, the church, including
you and me, is bereft of God's word.

Don't let such reasoning disarm you. You *do* have in your
hand the *graphē*, the inspired word of God, and it is worthy
of your trust and commitment. You have "the sword of the
Spirit." When you quote it, let your "thus saith the Lord" ring
with confident conviction.

Some would say this is deception, that this can be said
only of the autographs. It is *not* deception. It is true! The Bible
you hold in your hand *is* the word of God. Stand alone on it.
Bet your life on what it means. Hold it high in the air as you
sing with gusto the children's chorus, "The B-I-B-L-E." Proclaim with Jeremiah:

When your words came, I ate them;
   they were my joy and my heart's delight. . . .
                          (Jeremiah 15:16)

The meaning the Bible conveys *is inspired*. Digest it into your
mind and heart and life.

## You Are Responsible for Maintaining the Bible's Purity

Take time to revel in this celebration—all the time you like. Then, after you have satisfied your soul with its joy, sober up to the fact that pollution not only still resides there but is yet flooding in. Resolve to extricate as best you can what is there and to block as best you can what is coming in.

Finally, because you cannot avoid interpreting your Bible, do so with fear and trembling. Take off your shoes, for you are standing on holy ground. Stop polluting your Bible yourself, and don't tolerate anybody who does.

Conclusions, Notes

1. There are many other good English translations. For descriptions and evaluations, see John R. Kohlenberger III, *Words about the Word: A Guide to Choosing and Using Your Bible* (Grand Rapids, Mich.: Zondervan Publishing House, 1987) and Jack P. Lewis, *The English Bible/from KJV to NIV: A History and Evaluation* (Grand Rapids, Mich.: Baker Book House, 1981).

The *Eight Translation New Testament* available from Tyndale House Publishers, Inc. (Wheaton, Ill., 1974) places the New Testaments from four of my five nominees—the Jerusalem Bible, Today's English Version, the Revised Standard Version, and the New International Version—in parallel columns along with the New Testaments from the King James Version, the Living Bible, Phillips' New Testament in Modern English, and the New English Bible.